Fred Harrison was educated at Oxford and London universities. He worked for the *Sunday People* for 20 years, latterly as Chief Reporter handling major investigations. He is now a feature writer on *Today*. He edits a bi-monthly journal, *Land and Liberty* and is the author of a book on land use, *The Power in the Land*.

40/17

FRED HARRISON

Brady and Hindley

Genesis of the Moors Murders

GRAFTON BOOKS

A Division of the Collins Publishing Group

LONDON GLASGOW
TORONTO SYDNEY AUCKLAND

Grafton Books
A Division of the Collins Publishing Group
8 Grafton Street, London W1X 3LA

Published by Grafton Books 1987
Reprinted 1987 (twice)

First published in Great Britain by
Ashgrove Press Ltd 1986

Copyright © Fred Harrison 1986, 1987

ISBN 0-586-20002-9

Printed and bound in Great Britain by
Collins, Glasgow

Set in Baskerville

Acknowledgements

My thanks are due to Joseph Heller and Jonathan Cape Limited for permission to quote extracts from *Catch 22* and to the *Sunday People* for permission to reproduce the drawing of Ian Brady by Bob Williams.

Contents

Introduction

Ian Brady moved into 7 Bannock Street in June 1963 and became Myra Hindley's lover. A month later, he consecrated their relationship with the blood of 16-year-old Pauline Reade and began an affair that for 20 years has tormented the psyche of a nation.

Time has done nothing to diminish interest in the cold-blooded killings that received their name from the Yorkshire moors, where the bodies of children were buried in shallow graves in the acid peat. But the original revulsion for the Moors murderers has now been replaced by an unhealthy fascination with the case, a fascination that has generated myths that have no basis in reality. It is therefore important to reappraise what is still the most harrowing case of sadistic murder in modern British criminal history.

That – and the mystery of what happened to other children who disappeared in Manchester at the time – is the particular reason for re-opening the case. But there is another important justification: western society is afflicted with a new epidemic – homicidal tendencies towards children. In the psychiatrist's jargon, many of the killers lack "affect". That is, they are devoid of emotional feeling for their victims. Callous acts of murder with a gun or a knife, or by strangulation or other forms of brutal deprivation, are often perpetrated with the same air of detachment as, say, an act of personal hygiene.

But for society, the murder of children strikes at the soft underbelly of our collective emotions. For the killers are not visibly different from the rest of us. They are not "monsters" until they have been labelled as such by the media. How, then, can we identify them as separate from the rest of us? How can we be sure that *we* are not afflicted with the same fatal propensities? These are some of the painful questions that, all

11

too often, are hidden away behind public demonstrations of anger outside courthouses. While, all the time, more children are abducted, tortured and murdered.

The British, for example, who pride themselves in showing more love for animals than any other nation in the world, have the worst record in Europe for child murders. In the 10 years up to 1985, 1,997 children died from homicidal treatment, according to the best estimate by the National Society for the Prevention of Cruelty to Children.[1] That means an average of four children are dying from injuries, hunger, thirst, exposure and neglect every week. Three-quarters of these deaths are at the hands of parents or people in whose care the children have been placed. Is this an indictment of the way in which families rear those children who grow up to be child-killers? If so, how do those nurturing practices differ from the ones in use in nearly every home in the land?

In the United States the problem of cold-blooded murders has assumed the proportions of an epidemic. The negro is both the principal perpetrator and victim. For example, between July and November 1984, in Detroit, over 100 children under the age of 17 were shot; all but four were black. The leading cause of death among black men between the ages of 15 and 24 is murder by other blacks, and in most cases the motives seem to be irrational.

The dearth of well-researched evidence permits strong differences of opinion and prejudice to flourish as to why people kill. Theorists can proffer several reasons for the degeneration in social behaviour. Among them is the absence of a father-figure in one-parent families, which I suspect is very important. Significantly, nearly 60% of black children in America are born out of wedlock. "Most black children are now growing up without their fathers," according to the CBS documentary "The Vanishing Family – the Crisis in Black America", broadcast in January 1986. Poverty and the ghetto environment, as well as the despair generated by unemploy-

[1]Susan J. Creighton, 'Child Abuse Deaths', London: NSPCC, Information Briefing No. 5, October 1985.

ment, are also important factors. All of these contribute to the formation of nihilistic personalities, but a great deal more research needs to be undertaken before we can build up accurate profiles of child-killers which have predictive value (and which would therefore help us to prevent homicides).

The carnage in America is evidence enough of the urgent need for research. Senator Jesse Jackson put it this way: "We are losing more lives in the streets of America than we lost in the jungles of Viet Nam. We must be as serious about ending the war at home as the war abroad."[2] That we are not serious about dealing with the problem is evidenced by the fact that we do not even know how many children disappear from their homes each year. Such an elementary statistic is not available. In 1984, about 400 children who were recorded as missing on the Scotland Yard computer were not subsequently traced. This figure, however, is useless: it only takes in the London metropolitan area and a few other police forces in Britain. The Home Office, in acknowledging that comprehensive statistics on missing persons are not collected centrally, defends itself on the grounds that information for Great Britain as a whole "is available only at disproportionate cost". What price the loss of a child not just to its family but to a society that, outwardly at any rate, claims to be a caring one?

There is a similar statistical vacuum in the United States, where the best estimated data suggests that strangers abduct between 4,000 and 7,000 children a year.[3]

This gap in knowledge is indefensible. Government bureaucracies devote huge sums of money to the collection of data that is specifically designed to help the political lobbyists to milk the taxpayer's purse; yet on what is the most harrowing problem for thousands of families – the disappearance of one of their children, defenceless in an increasingly pitiless world – the authorities are unable even to define the size of the problem.

One way to mobilise the public agencies behind a more

2 'When Brother Kills Brother', *Time*, Sept. 16, 1985, p. 37.
3 'Missing Children: What Makes Search So Tough', *U.S. News & World Report*, Aug. 19, 1985, p. 61.

effective mechanism for tracing missing children is to remind ourselves that it can happen to any child, at practically any time. At present, the onus is placed almost exclusively on the children themselves. But while it is right to teach them not to accept sweets from strangers, far more needs to be done in crime prevention and detection. For example, there is considerable scope for improvement in what ought to be a simple matter – the exchange of information between police forces across territorial and administrative boundaries. And that is before we get down to the more difficult issue of appropriate changes in the law.

Above all else, however, social scientists should accelerate research into the nature of seemingly senseless killings. By understanding how and why children have died, we can help to prevent deaths in the future. That is why it is vital to understand the Moors murders, which in its extreme perversity and inhumanity makes it the classic study.

The principal purpose of this book, then, is to deepen our knowledge of the psycho-dynamics of cold-blooded murder. The search for the reasons why people mindlessly murder defenceless children must begin with an objective account of the biographies of the killers themselves, if we are to trace the course of causation back to its source.

* * *

My contact with Ian Brady began in 1983. I wrote a routine news report for the *Sunday People* about Ian Brady's health. His weight had dropped by 40 lbs in three years, to below 110 lbs. This suggested that he was suffering from a serious psychosomatic condition. Brady's prison visitor, Lord Longford, telephoned me to say that the story was exceptional for its accuracy, and he suggested that I should send a copy to Brady, who was in Gartree Prison, Leicestershire. This was the start of an exchange of letters that finally led me to solve two other child murders.

Throughout my subsequent investigation, I was reminded time and again that the British people are restless about – transfixed by – this case. I have now come to the conclusion that the explanation is a relatively simple one. People cannot *understand* those events in the early 1960s; they are hurt by the little that they know, and – without articulating the problem in these terms – they are searching for the answers to some deep-seated questions.

Most people can recall very few of the details, despite the high level of continuing media interest. They have vivid pictures in their minds of a brassy, hard-hearted blond called Myra who conspired with Ian Brady to torture and kill children. Above all, however, it is the tape-recording of the sadistic abuse of 10-year-old Lesley Ann Downey, a recording made while the child's body was being defiled, that keeps cutting away at the public's psyche.

The relationship between Ian Brady and Myra Hindley resulted in the deaths of at least five young people. Still, I could not convince myself that this was a sufficient explanation for the public's fixation. Other murderers have since matched or eclipsed their record of deaths Peter Sutcliffe prowled the dark streets of Yorkshire mill towns, killing 13 defenceless women in back alleys. Yet he, and others like him, have not attracted the kind of execration that is directed at Brady and Hindley. Their names are more quickly forgotten, while the name of Myra Hindley continues to evoke passion and pain. According to an opinion poll conducted by Audience Selection for the *Sun* (June 24, 1985), 86% of the public oppose parole for Hindley.

Even the names of child killers like Raymond Morris are forgotten, while Ian Brady's name evokes a special horror that is kept in check only because he constantly reassures the world that he does not ever wish to be granted his freedom.

None of the books that were published after the sensational trial at Chester Assizes in April 1966 provide the answers that we need if we are to finally put the case to rest. They were either expanded versions of newspaper reports, which presented the events as "murder-for-giggles";[4] or alternatively, they were unconvincing attempts to use the murders as part of a polemic against pornography[5]. Or, where time and trouble was taken to review the lives and times of the participants, fiction was used to ensure narrative continuity.[6]

So there was no comprehensive account. Why did an apparently normal, working class lass from Manchester allow herself to become involved in the sadistic torture of children? Was there a logic underpinning the rhythmic periodicity of the murders? Was the public right to suspect that Myra Hindley was the stronger, dominant member of the partnership? Was David Smith, the teenager who blew the whistle on Brady and Hindley, really the innocent victim portrayed by the prosecution at the trial? Did Brady and Hindley kill Pauline Reade and Keith Bennett? What happened to Philip Deare? Could it happen again?

At the outset I assumed that, after 20 years, the experts must have produced definitive answers to some of these questions. As one writer suggested in the *Sunday Telegraph* on May 8, 1966:

". . . ironically enough it is the Bradys and Hindleys who can take us further, if we have the wit to try and use them for that purpose while they are our captives. For just as it is for want of research that we know so little about how to stop gross sexual crime, so it must be through a proper study of the gross sexual deviate that we can start to remedy that situation."

It did not happen. Brady and Hindley were locked away in a penal system that courts silence behind the Official Secrets Act. I succeeded in penetrating that wall of secrecy on November 29, 1984. Ian Brady agreed to let me visit him. Because he was a Category A prisoner, I had to be vetted. The gates at Gartree were duly opened. Officialdom had failed to note that I was a

---

[4] John Deane Potter, *The Monsters of the Moors*, London: Elek, 1966, p. 12. See also David Marchbanks, *The Moors Murders*, London: Leslie Frewin, 1966, and Gerald Sparrow, *Satan's Children*, London: Odhams Books, 1966.

[5] Pamela Hansford Johnson, *On Iniquity*, London: Macmillan, 1967.

[6] Emlyn Williams, *Beyond Belief*, London: Hamish Hamilton, 1967.

journalist and author (even though I had written to Brady in both capacities, and the letters were subject to the censor's scrutiny). I was not, therefore, asked to sign a document promising to treat our conversations as confidential, and never to be disclosed to the public.

And so one of the Moors murderers – his mind tormented, his body seriously weakened – began the painful process of divulging his inner thoughts, the first British mass murderer to talk in the privacy of his cell to a writer about his terrible crimes. Brady could have died at any time, so brittle was his body and depressed his soul. I was racing against his biological clock. Slowly, in that darkened cavern, I began to understand the nature of evil. As individuals, there was little that was exceptional about Ian Brady and Myra Hindley; it was the synthesis of their personalities that created and unleashed a remorseless power which they could not control.

From Gartree, I visited the scenes where they committed their terrible deeds, the streets of Gorton, Hyde and Hattersley, where feelings run as high today as they ever did against Ian Brady, Myra Hindley – and David Smith. As I talked to the people in the streets and the council estates, I began to realise why ordinary people retained an abiding fascination with the Moors murders: fear. Fear underlies their anxiety about the case. Fear, not of the principal characters themselves; it is a fear generated by a failure to comprehend why it happened in the first place. Above all, the incomprehension about Myra Hindley's role: how could a woman offend against the protective maternal instinct that was nurtured into the genes in a process of evolution that spanned a period of two million years?

So the time has come for a new appraisal based on access to new information. My investigation was completed with mixed feelings. It gave me no pleasure to inform two mothers, Mrs Joan Reade and Mrs Winifred Johnson, in the Manchester office of the *Sunday People* on Saturday, June 29, 1985, that they could no longer continue to nurture the hope that still flickered in their lives, that their two children might still be alive.

But there was some satisfaction in developing answers to questions that have been gnawing away at the psyche of the British people for a generation. Brady and Hindley did not kill for kicks; I present an explanation in terms of a darker, deeper motivation. They created a cult; a killing cult. A volatile blend of psychopathic disorder and the love of a woman for a man served to nourish what Ian Brady now describes as "the rotten branch" of his life.

Cults built around a charismatic psychopath are alien to British society. They evolve more easily in California's drugs-based culture, where the pursuit of spiritual experiments around characters like Charles Manson have left their marks indelibly written in blood on the American nation's soul. Nonetheless, it did happen in Britain, a fact that has escaped attention. Ian Brady is what one psychiatrist who knows him well described as the Daddy of the Devils. If his behaviour can now be understood, we will have helped to exorcise the public's neurosis over the Moors murders.

But that is not to say that we should forget the evil deeds that began to come to light on October 7, 1965, the day on which Brady was arrested. When David Smith's six-month-old daughter, Angela Dawn, died early in 1965, the baby's aunt, Myra Hindley, sent a wreath to the funeral. On it was a message:

ANOTHER LITTLE FLOWER FOR GOD'S GARDEN
Myra

Brady and Hindley planted many flowers on the bleak moorlands of Yorkshire – their God's Garden. This book is dedicated to the memory of those flowers: Pauline, John, Lesley Ann, Keith and Edward.

PART ONE

Genesis

CHAPTER ONE

Psychopath

It was not an auspicious Sunday. Cold westerly winds had bellowed up the Clyde during the night, and the news vendor outside the gate of Rotten Row Maternity Hospital had repeatedly to stamp his feet on the frost-encrusted pavement to keep his blood circulating. The front page headline of the *Sunday Pictorial* attracted most attention: "Mona Tinsley's Spirit Led Her Slayer to Gallows". The police, desperately trying to solve the brutal murder of a 10-year-old girl, resorted to the use of a spiritualist to help them to track down the killer, Frederick Nodder.

Margaret Stewart, a 28-year-old tearoom waitress, gave birth to her illegitimate son on January 2, 1938. She christened him Ian Duncan Stewart. He was never to know his father. The unmarried mother rented a room in Caledonia Road, in the Gorbals, a tough inner city slum in Glasgow. But within a few months she realised that she could not cope with both a baby and a job. She advertised the need for someone to nurse her son, and Mrs May Sloan responded. She and her husband John loved children: they had two sons and two daughters of their own, all of them older than Ian. Between them they provided the little stranger with the security of a clean home, a brown-stone tenement in Camden Street.

Ian grew tall, thin and sallow. He was intellectually bright, but reluctant to apply himself to the full at Camden Street Primary School. He joined in the rough-and-tumble of street games, but he was shaping up into a lonesome character. He knew he was different. He did not know why; it was just a feeling that, somehow, he did not *belong*. He emphasised this apartness for the first time at Sunday school. The teacher asked: "Does everybody believe in God?" "No," came the reply from the sole dissenter. Ian was 5-years-old. Looking back on that incident, he identified it as the first occasion on which he chose to differentiate himself from his peers.

Ian's early experiments in cruelty were no different from the behaviour of many children who take delight in making animals suffer. He threw cats through windows to see if they could survive 30-foot falls and he killed his share of birds. But the little boy was not yet beyond the pale.

He was eight-years old when he suffered his first trauma. He was walking along one of the cobbled streets near home on a cold and frosty morning. His attention was attracted by a commotion, and he ran to see what the excitement was all about. Behind a gathering crowd was a sight of suffering that left its mark indelibly printed on the boy's emotions. A giant Clydesdale, which was pulling a drayman's cart, had slipped on the cobbles and had broken a bone. It was in agony. Ian felt helpless as the majestic beast appealed to him for relief from the searing pain: it stared at him, screaming silently through two large pools of water-filled eyes. Ian could not stand the sight of the stricken beast. He ran away, tears streaming down his cheeks.

The overriding emotion in Ian Stewart's early boyhood years was one of a strange emptiness. The Sloan family kept him warm and well-fed, and life revolved around the routines of school and play, seasonal festivities and pocket-knife adventures in the streets. The tenement blocks marked the territorial boundaries of his world, protecting his body and yet, in some indefinable way, imprisoning his soul. Then, during his ninth year, Mrs Sloan announced a treat: the family was going to the country for the day. She packed sandwiches, and they set off for the hills around Loch Lomond. It was the fatal turning point in Ian Stewart's life.

The boy was entranced by the vast open space. He felt the mystical calls of nature all around him, and he wondered. He knew instantly that he had an affinity with whatever was out there, beckoning him, trying to liberate his soul. He felt nature's power pulsing around him as he climbed, a solitary figure, higher up the hillsides. He stood motionless for an hour as the strength of nature coursed through his body. The howling wind and the thorny heather, the clouds bellowing through the heavens – this was where Ian belonged. It was a spiritual experience, the origins of the boy's pantheism, which affirms the unity of the gods with nature itself.

Intuitively, the boy knew that he was not one of the Sloans. They succoured him, but theirs' was not his natural home. Now he had found the spiritual comfort he needed, which filled the emotional vacuum of his childhood. The formative events started to come thick and fast.

When Ian reached the age of 12, his dog became ill. He prayed to God that his pet would not die. His prayers went unanswered, which convinced Ian that there was no personal God. A year later, he discovered that he was born a bastard. It was the crushing news that confirmed that he was an outsider, and he turned his back on society. He sought fulfilment in petty crime, and escaped the realities of life in the fantasy of the cinema. House-breaking and burglary did not pay: he was caught and brought before the juvenile courts. His behaviour was treated as the tearaway misdemeanours of a working class lad from the slums, pranks out of which he would grow with the passage of time.

Then, one day, he was at the end of his school career. He scanned the job advertisements in the local Press, and finally found one that looked promising. He mounted his bicycle outside the Sloan's house in Templeland Road, Pollock, an overspill estate on the outskirts of Glasgow, and rode through the Hillingdon housing estate on his way to an interview. As he turned a corner, Ian felt giddy. He dismounted, and stood in the doorway of a newsagent's shop. His head was spinning. He supported himself by leaning against the newsagent's window. And there it was, a green, warm radiation, not unattractive to the young man who clutched his head to try and steady himself. The features were unformed, but still recognisable. Ian knew that he was looking at The Face of Death. He did not know, on that rain-swept day in Glasgow, that this experience was destined to become the focus of his private cult; that the souls of innocent children would be sacrificed to The Face of Death. But he instantly knew that his salvation was irrevocably bound to its demands. "I'll do it a favour, and – like it will do, in the end – it will do me favours." The bond with death was fused by that green radiation.

* * *

One of Ian's first jobs was butcher's assistant. He saw the sharp knife being wielded dispassionately against flesh and bone. What could be done to dead meat could be done to live flesh: on at least one occasion, he joined a gang of youths to carve up a 16-year-old boy with knives.

The fantasy of life as an outcast from a society that he despised now consumed his thoughts. He was going to be the Master criminal. In the meantime he settled for small-time housebreaking expeditions. He fell foul of the police on several occasions. After one sortie, a boy made the mistake of informing on him. Years later, when he moved to Manchester, he told the story of his revenge. He boasted that he had murdered the boy and buried him on a bomb-site in the Gorbals[1]. Nobody believed him. The world was yet to learn that Ian Stewart was a young man who did not lie.

He was due for his third term of probation for house-breaking and theft a few weeks before the age of 17 when officialdom struck its first deep blow. Ian could stay out of prison if he went to live with his mother in Manchester.

Mrs Sloan was bewildered at the way in which Ian had turned out. He was now beyond her control, and she agreed to his departure. The youth had no alternative, and his mother, Mrs Brady – she had moved south and married by this time – accepted her son into her home in December 1954. It was a traumatic experience for Ian. The welcome from his natural

---

[1] Potter, *op cit.*, p. 206.

mother did not compensate for the loss of his familiar surroundings in Glasgow. He retained an affection for the Sloan family, and Scotland would forever remain his home territory. For now, however, he was a misfit in an English city, a gangly youth with a broad accent from north of the border and poor prospects.

Ian was searching for an identity. Like other youngsters at this age – let alone one who found himself in a strange environment – he needed to define his role in society and discover his unique space in the universe. Emotionally, he was rootless. But to start with, he had to establish himself with a new name: Brady. He appeared to settle down quickly, working as a porter at the Smithfield market until he was arrested on January 10, 1956, for stealing lead seals. Borstal "training" took the form of two years being locked away with the criminal fraternity, learning some of the advanced tricks of the lock-picking trade.

His first stop was a camp of wooden huts at Hatfield, Yorkshire. At the end of his first year, however, he got drunk on home-brewed hooch and was transferred to the tighter security of a borstal in Hull, on the east coast. Here, he was interviewed by a psychiatrist, who rejected him as unsuitable for National Service.

Psychiatrists now say that, by the age of 17, Ian Brady was psychopathic. His personality had set into a hard, cold mould that was empty of all human feeling. But the inadequate state of psychiatric knowledge at the time meant that the personality tests to which the youth was subjected were incapable of predicting that he constituted a risk to society and was in urgent need of corrective therapy. Even today, medical science cannot offer a satisfactory explanation for the way in which Brady's personality began to disintegrate in his middle teens. All we can say is that the unique combination of genetic, social and environmental influences provided the necessary ingredients.

In retrospect, we can see the direction in which the formation of Brady's character was going. According to one confidential psychiatric report, written many years later:

"At the time of his sentence he felt that this was a time of deep crisis in his life and that in some way a decision had been made. He felt increasingly cut off from other people in the emotional sense – he could no longer feel concern for them or feel warmly towards them. He retained affection for his foster family.

"He found an affinity for literature of a sadistic nature and had sympathy with fascist ideology and Nazi practices. He says he was exhilarated by their loss of feeling, as it appeared as a liberation or freedom but at the same time he was distressed."

In captivity, society could have studied Brady carefully. By anticipating the kind of behaviour that could reasonably be expected of a psychopath, appropriate controls and remedial help could have been provided. This opportunity was lost, however, and – a generation later – the same criticism can be levelled at the way dangerous people are allowed to slip through the nets that are supposed to protect society from the mass killers of children.[2]

Before his release from borstal, Brady carefully filed away a list of names of inmates whom he thought would be useful to him in his career as a big-time crook. He made sure that he had a contact in every major town in the north of England. He needed access to people who were experts in safe-breaking, or driving getaway cars. He returned to Manchester on November 14, 1957, armed with the knowledge of some slick tricks that would help him to get rich quick. But he was not yet

[2] A recent example is that of Sandra Riley. Born an illegitimate child, she was adopted at the age of two months. Her first child, a girl, was illegitimate, and was adopted. She then married, and had four sons. The first died six weeks after its birth, in January 1975, allegedly of cot syndrome. Her two sons born in 1981 and 1983 were both suffocated to death by their mother. She pleaded guilty to infanticide, and was placed on probation. During her treatment, psychiatrists failed to detect that she was a psychopath. Eighteen months after being placed on probation, she drowned her 8-year-old son in the bath. On January 9, 1986, at Chester crown court, she was committed to a secure mental hospital for an indefinite period.

ready to go into top-gear in his chosen profession. Brady had a restless mind that needed educating. He needed a philosophy that would give direction to his life. It was while he was in this suggestive frame of mind that he visited the public library at Longsight, soon after his return to Manchester. There, he borrowed the alluringly titled *Crime and Punishment*.

In 1865 Fyodor Dostoyevsky (1821-1881) wrote what was to become one of the great Russian classics. It was a story about Raskolnikov, a penniless student in Moscow who conceived a plan to get money: kill the old woman usurer who charged high rates of interest for the money she loaned to the needy.

Murder? "Listen," Raskolnikov told Sonia, "I wanted to become a Napoleon – that's why I killed the old woman. Well, do you understand now?"

Sonia did not fully understand the meaning of the words she heard. Was Raskolnikov really telling her that he had murdered an old woman? So Raskolnikov patiently explained:

"You see, what happened was that one day I asked myself this question: what if Napoleon, for instance, had been in my place and if he had not had a Toulon or an Egypt or the crossing of Mont Blanc to start his career with, but instead of all those splendid and monumental things, there had simply been some ridiculous old woman, the widow of some low-grade civil servant, who had, in addition, to be murdered to get the money from her box (for his career, of course). Well, would he have made up his mind to do it if there was no other way? Would he too have felt disgusted to do it because it was far from monumental and – and wicked, too? Well, let me tell you, I spent a long, long time worrying over that 'question', so that in the end I felt terribly ashamed when it occurred to me (quite suddenly, somehow) that he wouldn't have felt disgusted at all and that indeed it would never have occurred to him that it was not monumental. In fact, he would not have understood what there was to be so squeamish about. And if he had had no other alternative, he would have strangled her without the slightest hesitation, and done it thoroughly, too. Well, so I, too, hesitated no longer and – and murdered her – following the example of my authority. And that's exactly how it was. You think it's funny? Well, yes, the funny part about it, Sonia, is that that's exactly how it was."[3]

For Ian Brady, the warped logic that Raskolnikov employed to justify murder was a perfect fit for his crippled personality. Here, in black and white, articulated by one of the greatest authors of all time, was the creed that washed away the lingering doubts about the morality of murder. Evocatively presented by the Russian master, the Napoleonic thesis was one of the last pieces to be fitted into the fatal jigsaw of experiences that shaped Ian Brady's behaviour.

* * *

Brady was experiencing what psychiatrists call " a profound affective change" of the sort that can be found in people suffering from schizophrenia. This means that he was rapidly losing the capacity for normal human emotions. He could not feel sorry for people; pain caused no anguish in his soul. He was, in his own mind, superior to those who allow their feelings to dictate their behaviour – feelings that prevent mere mortals from inflicting pain on others. He was now in the Napoleonic mould, and *nothing* – least of all common morality – could stop him. Kill, if necessary: there are no constraints on The Great Ones.

Both psychologically and socially, Ian Brady was marooned on an island of private emotions, the architect of fantastic deeds. He despised men who accepted self-imposed limits to their behaviour, limits which were ultimately dictated by the elites who manipulated people for their own ends. Morality, he

[3] Fydor Dostoyevsky, *Crime and Punishment*, translator: David Magarshack, Harmondsworth: Penguin Books, 1951, pp. 428–9.

learned from his study of Nazi philosophy, was relative; the victor decided what was acceptable behaviour, and the vanquished were not entitled to appeal for protection from universally valid principles of truth and justice.

Death was Ian Brady's constant companion. It lurked in his head, and it found its brutal expression in the backstreets, where he clubbed people to death. These were random acts of homicide which gave him no spiritual satisfaction. They were products of a deep torment, the result of a loss of self-control.

But he knew that, one day, he would convert his homicidal acts into deeds of monumental proportions. That would happen when he was ready to escape from the dark shadows of his mind and intrude on the real world. All the essential elements were in place for his venture into immortality. His character was deformed: there had been no paternal strong hand to pull him back from the abyss, no natural family to bond him to the warmth and security that a child needs. He became introspective in thought, secretive in behaviour, and Raskolnikov provided the philosophy that would one day enable him to match Napoleon himself.

And he had discovered his spiritual home. He was liberated from the torments in his soul by the open spaces of nature. He had moulded his character against the granite rocks of the Scottish highlands. It was on a trip to Glencoe, in Argyllshire, that the boy discovered what he perceived to be the mystical qualities of Rannoch Moor. The Face of Death lived here. The root of the word "moor" is generally held by scholars to be connected with the word meaning "to die".[4] So the word was applied to dead or barren land, a perfect description of Rannoch Moor. The highly acidic waters, in pools and streams on plateaux generally between 1,200 feet and 2,200 feet above sea level, are poor in basic ions, especially calcium. This, felt Ian, was where he was free of the troubles of the world, where he could soothe his mind and escape the petty constraints of the society that had abandoned him at birth.

[4] A. G. Tansley, *The British Islands and their Vegetation*, Vol. II, Cambridge University Press, pp. 674–4.

The move to Manchester left him gulping like a fish coming to the surface for oxygen. He felt trapped and suffocated in the mosaic of red-brick terraced houses. To relieve the claustrophobia, he regularly visited the tearooms in the railway stations, to daydream as he watched the endless stream of travellers throbbing through the terminals. Then, one day, blessed relief: he, too, could go on a journey. He bought a silver Tiger Cub motorcycle. Its 250cc engine was good enough for pottering about the city, but one of his first journeys was north-eastwards through Ashton under Lyne, a small market town, and into open country along the A.635. Suddenly, he was on Saddleworth Moor. He was back home. He instantly recognised the common cottongrass which is associated with acid bogs. The plant, which colonises the cracks in peat, is distinguished by the silky flower heads that look like small clumps of wool torn off the back of sheep, the only creatures capable of surviving on this barren landscape.

The desolation of Saddleworth Moor matched Ian Brady's soul. The lashing, biting winds were as merciless as his tungsten steel heart. The acid in the peat was as corrosive as the blood that coursed through his veins. His secretive nature reflected the sterile terrain, and his dark moods echoed from the shifting black peat which cautioned the travellers from Barnsley against venturing off the road.

High on the moors, Brady could inhale the ferment of death which was carried by the gusts of wind that swept across nature's cemetery. Here was the home of his god. The Face of Death could swallow the bodies of mortal men, corrode them with acid and leave no trace. Here, Ian Brady knew that he would one day deliver his sacrifices, to keep faith with the vow he took that day in Glasgow when he was initiated into the secrets of the spirit world. This would be his Napoleonic deed: he would reap his salvation with human sacrifices.

But something was missing.

No man can remain an island for long: he must eventually reach out and seek a place in the real world. In doing so, he tests his self-image, and defines his identity. This transforms fantasy into fact. Ian Brady needed his Sonia, someone whom he could initiate into his secret, someone whom he could trust to bear witness to his heroism. Where was she?

CHAPTER TWO

Street Fighter

Joyce Hull was a handsome lady. She had dark hair and well-painted lips, and she liked to make the best of a rationed life in those early postwar years. Money was short, so there were no fancy clothes to be worn during a night out at the pub. Still, she knew how to wear a pretty headscarf and cheap brooch to liven up her appearance.

On January 9, 1948, she gave birth to a boy in Withington Hospital, Manchester. The child was christened David Hull. Within two years his mother was gone. Sometime later when he was old enough to understand, he was told that she had died. He was taken in by his paternal grandparents, Annie and John Smith, who lived in Aked Street, Ardwick. Annie became David's "mum".

Aked Street, close to the centre of Manchester, was two rows of Victorian terraced houses. No 39 was cosy and clean; the large fire range in the living room was regularly buffed up, to keep it shining. Unlike many other families who occupied the two-up, two-downs built by the local slumlords at the turn of the century, the Smith's home had a bathroom inside the house.

Annie Smith had five children of her own, one of whom was David's father, John. The children were all off her hands when David arrived. The baby was legally adopted by his grandparents, a fact that was kept secret from the neighbours. John, a maintenance fitter, travelled the country in the course of his work, and rarely visited his son.

Annie Smith was a proud woman, tall and thin-faced, with a pointed nose and weak chin. She enjoyed dressing in the fashion of the day. Her hair was kept in a permanent wave, the style of the '50s, and she wore tailored dresses with pleats and suede court shoes. She even had the occasional use of a fur jacket, which was well above the norm for someone who worked as a cleaner at the Royal Infirmary.

Annie's relationship with her husband was a strained one. John Smith was a gambler who, it seemed to young David, did not show enough respect for his hard-working wife. Consumer goods were used as stake money in the gaming houses of Blackpool, the Lancashire holiday resort to which John Smith paid regular visits. He would hire a furniture van and head for the coast. If his luck was in, he returned with a three-piece suite, or fur coats. Annie sported the coats until John found himself locked into a losing streak; then the prized possessions ended up in a pawn shop. Money came and went fast. Kim, the family pet dog, kept company with a shoe box in the cubby hole beneath the stairs which was often stashed full of pound notes.

Annie slept in the second-floor attic with David, while her husband occupied one of the two bedrooms. She loved the little boy, and he became her co-conspirator. Annie claimed that she did not drink, but David knew otherwise. He was the one who went to the local shop to buy the bottles of Guinness for "me mum" and he hid them behind the stove, so that no-one would discover Annie's secret.

The early years were good. The Smith family always congregated at No 39 for Christmas celebrations. The cupboard was filled with home-made mince pies, and the turkey was done to a treat in the big fire range. The community spirit had not yet been wiped out by the City Corporation's slum-clearance programme, so Guy Fawkes night was a street affair. The big bonfire was built in the middle of the road, and the children had their share of fun with the bangers and the fluorescent cartwheels and candles which showered out their psychedelic puffs of smoke.

Auntie Betty and Uncle Albert lived two doors away, so David played with cousins Frank, John and Graham. David knew that, compared with them, he was spoilt. His mum would leave two-bob pieces with his bag of sweets. The money he reclaimed when he returned the empty bottles of Guinness went straight into his pocket, and would be spent on bars of chocolate.

David never stole from his mum, but he was not averse to relieving his grandfather of the occasional half-crown. Grandfather Smith soon got wise to the boy's habit, however, and began counting his change when he went to bed. In the morning, if he found one of the coins missing, David received "an awful leathering".

Ross Place School was at the end of Aked Street, so David did not have far to travel. He soon acquired a reputation for being "cock of the class", but in the early years there was no indication of uncontrollable violence. At lunchtimes, he lined up in the free meals queue. David was delighted that he was able to get more on his plate – and second helpings! – than the children whose parents paid for their meals.

Not that food was a problem for David; his mum made sure of that. She had a knack of making lacklustre food seem exciting. For example, Saturday night de-lousing sessions were ritual events that could be anticipated with pleasure. The cod liver oil and syrup of figs were acceptable because there appeared to be a limitless supply of dark chocolates at the end of it all. His mum omitted to tell him that the chocolate had remarkable laxative qualities.

The only confusion in David's early years occurred during his seventh year. His father began to make regular Sunday afternoon trips to Aked Street. John James Smith, a tall, slim man who wore glasses, was a misogynist. Why he hated women is not clear, but he used to say that a woman's fortune was between her legs. He did not have much time for children, either, but out of the blue the visits to Belle Vue zoo began. He arrived after the pubs closed, reeking of beer. Occasionally, he arrived with a treat, like a plastic guitar. Father and son caught the bus to Belle Vue, where David stared in wonder at the lions and tigers. By now, he knew that the man who held his hand was his father, but that did not stop him from regarding his grandmother as his mum.

The visits to the zoo continued for two years. Then, just as suddenly, John Smith slipped out of his son's life. That did not upset the boy too much; he had all the love and security he needed from his mum, and his tough-boy status made sure that he did not have to actually fight to retain his reputation as cock of the class.

The classroom routines were no trouble to David Smith, who seemed to have a gift for English composition. Over the years, however, a vague uneasiness had crept in which one day found expression in what seemed to be an innocent question – one which was to have unforeseeable consequences for the boy's happiness.

He asked his mum: "Why am I getting free dinners?"

The Smiths of Aked Street were not exactly on the poverty line, so they could have afforded to pay for the lunchtime meals.

For some months his mum was evasive. Something was evidently troubling her about the answer, so she avoided the issue until the boy was in his tenth year.

Then it came out: "Because your mum's not dead."

So far as the education authorities were concerned, David Smith was the son of a one-parent family, which entitled him to free school meals.

The boy went berserk. He kicked his mum's shins, hard and often. The kicking continued for two solid hours. He lashed out, crying and screaming, until he had exhausted himself. Then, his mum took him into the kitchen. Her shins were red raw. She faced the boy against a wall, and whipped him with a strip of rubber from an old pram wheel. The rubber had two steel threads running through it. The boy took his beating: "She had her pound of flesh".

But his mum now became "Mrs Smith". For months he remained hostile to the woman whom he loved. He refused to accept dinners at school, so his grandmother had to give him two-bob pieces to buy fish and chips. That was more than enough to buy some cigarettes as well. David began to smoke. He also became unruly in the classroom, and he started fighting the form prefects.

The boy's identity had been wrenched away from him. It was not his grandmother's fault, but David Smith's anger smouldered for six months. Life at 39 Aked Street could never be the same again. Even so, it still provided him with the security of a home. Within a few months of discovering that he was a bastard, however, he suffered another crushing blow. John Smith arrived home late one night, and engaged in an argument with his parents. David was in bed, and did not know what was happening until his father stormed into the attic.

"Come on, son, we're going," he said as he clutched David's arm.

The boy grabbed his white giraffe, and in nothing but his pyjamas he was hustled outside to a taxi. David's grandmother was crying. The black taxi moved off from No 39. It was only a 10-minute drive down Hyde Road, a left turn into Cambert Lane opposite the town hall, left again into Taylor Street, and left again into the small rabbit warren of red-brick houses where John Smith was living in lodgings. The taxi drew up outside 13 Wiles Street, Gorton. David Smith's nightmare had begun.

* * *

No 13 was at the end of the cul-de-sac. Its retaining wall butted onto the side of the railway track, so the house was regularly suffused with the white smoke that billowed up the bank from the locomotives.

David was shown into a lice-ridden bed. The peeling plaster on the ceiling formed the shapes of disfigured faces.

Elizabeth Jones, in whose house he was now a lodger, came into David's bedroom early the next morning. For the first time, he saw the large ugly cyst on the left side of her head. The boy was horrified, and he took an immediate dislike to the frail little spinster. His father could not console him, but it was made perfectly clear that he could not return to "me mum".

The dark, pokey hole in Wiles Street was now his home. The cast-iron range in the front room was dull and greasy, for want of elbow grease. For a bath, David had to visit Gorton Baths where 6d bought him the use of a towel and a cube of soap.

No amount of soap could wash away his distress. His mother was not really his mother, and now his home was not his home. All the bonds were destroyed. The world was against David Smith, and he was going to go down fighting.

At first, it was Miss Jones who bore the brunt of his aggression. On more than one occasion he kicked her down the stairs. "I hated the woman. I had been taken from a gentle, white-haired lady and handed over to something with a dirty big cyst on her head. She used to go to the Steel Works Tavern and come back drunk: she gave me a shilling each time, so that I wouldn't tell me dad, but that was no consolation for what I had to live with."

Arrangements were made for David to go to the Cummings' house for breakfast. Clara and George Cummings were a kindly couple with a large family of seven sons and five daughters who lived at No 1 Benster Street. After breakfast, David made the journey back to Ross Place School.

The teachers noticed a serious deterioration in the boy's behaviour. One day, he was caught squabbling with Tony Jackson on the cricket field. They were separated, and the school was lined up to form a boxing ring. The gloves were taken out of the cupboard and placed on the hands of the two boys. David Smith did not have any doubt that he could lick Tony Jackson in a bare-knuckle contest. Leather gloves and rules changed his prospects, and Jackson won on points. "I don't think I laid a punch on him, on that occasion. It was too technical for me. They even had a referee!"

John Smith bought a tortoise, which was named Joey. David's demeanour was not improved, however, when Miss Jones' dog, Minnie, bit off the creature's head.

More harrowing than that, however, was an incident that left its mark on David for a long time. A distant relative of Miss Jones' occasionally came to stay. Because there were only two bedrooms, he had to share a bed with David. One night, the man began to fondle the boy. David's throat went dry. He lay motionless, pretending to be asleep and unaware of the man's caresses.

At school, the children in their final year were preparing for the 11-plus examination, which would determine whether they went to a grammar or secondary modern school. The rebellious David Smith was not cooperative. His world had been wrecked, anyway, so why bother to pass exams? He was expected to pass his English test. For his composition, however, he took two minutes to write down the lyrics of a Ray Charles song. He turned the paper face down, in defiance, and stood his ground against authority. He had begun the brutal process of stripping himself of self-respect. He did not like the image that fate had bestowed upon him – a rootless bastard living in a filthy house – so he set about establishing a new identity for himself, one which he would be solely responsible for creating. His break with the past occurred one cold morning in 1959.

David rose from his bed and could not find a clean shirt. He complained to his father, who reacted angrily. John Smith picked up a dog chain and struck his son over the back. David clenched his right fist and struck his father in the face. Father and son rained blows down on each other, and eventually the older man was lying on the floor, conquered by his son.

The police were called. David was sent to Rose Hill Remand Home for a brief spell. That did not worry him: he was a hard man, now. Years later, however, he realised what a terrible price his father had paid. "I broke his spirit. It was a dumb thing to do to your father; you should not do it to your father at any age – but remember, I was only a kid, which made it even worse. I should not have won that fight. I never lost one after that."

* * *

David Smith rapidly shaped up into a hard case, so it was a stroke of good luck that the Manchester education authorities decided to send him to Stanley Grove School, in Longsight, for his secondary education. Mr Sidney Silver, the headmaster, ran a boxing school. He soon discovered that David Smith, who had performed well in several inter-school bouts, was a natural fighter. He was entered for the school championships, and he battled his way through to the finals at the Kings Hall, Belle Vue. Smith fought a boy called Willatt. They were trained at Stretford Boys Club, which used a room in the local police station as a gym. It was a hard fight, and Smith won. His father, who was at the ringside, was elated. As a reward, he bought the boy a pair of boxing boots.

Now David Smith was a champion. He acquired new self-respect and a new identity. He was able to ventilate his aggression in a socially-approved manner, cajoled on by the masters in his corner of the ring. "I thumped hell out of them, and it was legitimate. The masters were encouraging me to get stuck in there, with both gloves, according to the Queensberry Rules, but I just wanted to hammer my opponents with my right fist."

Smith was selected to represent Manchester against Oldham, in the 11-12 years age bracket. It was to be his last fight in the ring.

Who can say what the little hero's destiny would have been, had he followed through with a career in the ring? As it was, his mum – his grandmother was by now back in favour – told him to give it up. Boxing, she warned him, would leave him with a cauliflower ear. When his mum told him to do something, he did it. Mr Silver was angry, but he could not persuade the boy to put the gloves back on.

After that, it seemed to David that the teachers picked on him. They always had an excuse, because David infringed the school rules on what was an appropriate uniform. He liked to wear tight jeans, black T-shirts or black shirts with the collars turned up, and winkle picker shoes. David Smith chose to model himself on the sultry James Dean look, which was fashionable. And hadn't Eddie Cochran just died? His loss to pop music was of greater consequence to David Smith than the sartorial preferences of stuffy Sidney Silver.

He was sent home at least five times. His father sent him back in baggy trousers, but David took a needle and thread to stitch up the legs while riding the No 53 bus up Kirkhamshulme Lane.

The inevitable finally happened. He was told to report to Mr Silver. The headmaster tried to admonish the surly boy, who glared back with dumb insolence in his eyes, then swivelled round and made for the door. Mr Silver leapt to his feet, and David thumped him once. That ended all hope of a return to legitimate fighting. Smith was expelled.

He now turned to street fighting. He adopted the image of the Rocker, sporting the regulation T-shirt and leather motorcycle jacket, his jet-black hair heavily greased with Loxene. Smith, now known by the nickname of Smogger, went looking for fights. He knew that the best way to get on top and stay there without having to engage in too many fist-fights was to develop the reputation of a hard man. He grasped every opportunity to straighten out a situation with his fists. On one occasion, for example, he spotted a friend being "touched up by a dirty old man" in the Essoldo, in Mount Road, the Taylor Street boys' cinema. "I leathered him, butted him with my head and in the end the management had to be called to stop us. My friend went out and told his friends that I had helped him. That protected me for a few weeks."

The Marquess of Queensberry held no sway in the streets of Gorton, where – in David Smith's view – there were just two rules. One was that you never turned your back on the enemy, particularly when walking away from a fight. The other one was that you *never* lost a fight. If necessary you stayed on top by using a blunt instrument. Percy Waddington discovered that when, in the playground of All Saint's School in Gorton Lane, he called David a bastard. "It was the free dinner ticket coming back at me." He picked up a cricket bat and broke the boy's fingers; he was then expelled.

Anyone who wanted to test his prowess against David Smith only had to insult him. One favourite way was to call him "One Tit", a nickname which he acquired after his mum had a cancerous breast removed.

The mothers of the Taylor Street boys despaired at Smith, who did not seem to respond to the direst threats. Mrs Patricia Hamnett was one of them. She used to voice her complaints to old Granny Maybury, one of her neighbours who lived two doors up in Bannock Street with her granddaughter Myra. Mrs Hamnett's two sons, Chris and Arthur, played with Dave Smith. When Smith acquired an air pistol, he thought nothing of shooting lead pellets at the acne-faced Chris as they played on the crofts, the pieces of wasteland that separated their streets. "I used to go to Dave Smith's house with a knife to frighten him," says Mrs Hamnett, "but he just swore at me. It was a waste of time mythering over him."

Smith was not unbeatable in a fair fight: he could sometimes be flattened. His adversaries always made the mistake of turning their backs on him as they walked away. That was all that Smith needed to pick up a brick and strike from the back. "There was no point in being beaten, because you lost everything, in them days. You might get the best hiding, but the other boy would not be able to claim he was walking at the end of it. If he was walking away, you had to get up and use a brick on him. Otherwise, other boys would come looking for you."

Humiliating a boy who was a prospective threat was a technique that Smith perfected. Winning a verbal argument was not enough. "I would then smack him in the mouth, and unless he hit back, there was no way he would retaliate in the future."

Boys who were not street-wise but carried weapons soon found themselves in trouble. "One lad came at me with a cut-throat razor," recalls Smith. "I caught his wrist, and he made the mistake of letting the blade wobble loose instead of locking it into the handle. I closed the blade over the top of his fingers, cutting the backs of his fingers.

"You didn't carry weapons to use as tooth-picks. I carried knives to use them. It didn't matter if you met a hard man; he just would not win. I used the weapon properly on him. I was not 'into' guys who carried weapons who wouldn't use them. I carried a weapon because I knew I was going to be beaten up. But sure as hell that did not mean I was going to lose the fight. I might fight a person twice my size, but he was going to lose.

"You could protect yourself with a reputation. If you stuck two people with knives, others avoided you: so you carried blades. You were creating a head banger impression to frighten people off. Your reputation increased if you got away with it, and were not prosecuted."

David Smith did not escape prosecution altogether. He appeared before the courts twice on assault and wounding charges. The first occasion was at the age of 11, and it happened again four years later.

His third appearance was on July 8, 1963, when he was put on probation for three years for housebreaking and larceny, and storebreaking and larceny. He and Sammy Jepson, who lived near the chip shop in Taylor Street, stole electrical goods such as kettles and blankets. At the time, he and Sammy were good mates. David would never have dreamt that, two years later, he would help his new friend Ian Brady to compile a murder list with Sammy's name at the top of it.

CHAPTER THREE

The Gorton Girls

It took five generations to create the network of blood ties and territorial allegiances that established the working class solidarity of Gorton. Although construction of the Gorton Cotton Mill started in 1824, the Mill did not come into production until 20 years later. The major turning point in local fortunes – measured in particular by booming land values – was in 1848, when construction of the principal buildings of the Sheffield and Manchester Railway began. These included the wagon and locomotive repair shops. The works eventually covered 50 acres, and Gorton became the premier base for train drivers: they had the pick of the best paid routes.

By the turn of the century Gorton also boasted a cotton factory, chemical and iron works and a tanyard. It was a typical working class district, its rows of jerry-built dwellings punctuated here and there by the factories of heavy industry. On the surface, it was all drudgery. Day in and day out, the men donned their cloth caps and set off with their lunchboxes under their arms. The women shouldered their share of the burden of the industrial revolution, by feeding and reproducing the families that provided the new generations for the work-benches.

So far as the social planners of the 1950s were concerned there was little that was exceptional about life in the maze of Victorian slums that was worth preserving. In fact, what they saw they did not like at all. That was why the town councillors sent in the bull-dozers, to clear the red-brick rabbit warrens that were homes to thousands of families.

But the heavy artillery did more than pull down the wretched buildings that lacked basic amenities. It also destroyed the ligaments of a social framework that anchored people in familiar surroundings. The idea of reconstructing the communities while the families remained *in situ* was a concept that had to wait until Prince Charles popularised it 30 years later. The fad of the '50s was to destroy, and the Cummings family of Benster Street was a prime target for the social engineers who advocated a brave New World of skyscraper blocks and sterilised council estates on greenfield sites far from the madding crowd. George Cummings, who had TB, did not work. His wife, Clara, worked occasionally at the local pie factory and gave birth to one child every year for 12 years – seven boys and five girls.

Benster was one of eight streets that coagulated into a social unit: it linked to Wiles, Timothy, Charmers, the southern end of Preston, Bannock and Eaton streets, which radiated off the top end of the road that gave the local boys' gang its name, Taylor Street. This organic complex was bounded on the north by Gorton Lane, and on the south side by "posh" Furnival Road, a street of private residences. To the west was a croft and the main railway line running up to Piccadilly Station, three miles away, and on the east side was the Casson Street recreation ground. Here, hemmed in by clearly defined social and geographical boundaries, the first postwar generation was reared.

"I don't know why they called it a slum," says Pat, the eldest daughter in the Cummings family. "None of the houses was scruffy inside, and we used to clean the streets and each other's steps. People laugh at me now when I tell them we even used to sweep the croft behind our house, which was a barren piece of land with no grass, just hard soil."

Life was certainly cramped in No 1, Benster Street. "Six of us used to sleep in one bed," recalls Pat, "so we were always warm and cosy! I became the second mother to my brothers and sisters. We had to do things by clockwork. For example, Sundays was bath day. I would bring in the tin bath from outside, heat up the water in a gas boiler, and transfer the water with a bucket. We would start in the afternoon, one by one until the last one had his bath in the evening. We were crowded out, but we were happy."

Despite the shortage of income and space, the front door of the Cummings home was always open. Young David Smith was a regular at the breakfast table with the others who were getting ready for school. Bread and dripping was a modest meal, but it kept you going until lunchtime.

The Cummings children were generally well behaved. The worst "spot of bother" that any of them got into was when one of the younger boys became involved in an argument with David Smith from Wiles Street, the local tearaway who was always settling disputes with knuckles and knives. Smith got the upper hand in a brawl. Dennis, the eldest boy, waded in with his fists. Smith was carrying a bowie knife. He plunged the thick blade into Dennis' groin, shoved the blood-smeared knife down an onlooker's jumper and slouched off with his hands deep in his pockets.

* * *

The girls of Gorton were of hardy stock. The most timid of them was probably Pauline Reade, who lived with her brother Paul two doors away from David Smith in Wiles Street. As far as the boys of Taylor Street were concerned, in her early teenage years Pauline was definitely unwilling to share her sexual favours with them at this early stage in her life. She had experimented with a few kissing sessions with David, and they talked about going out together; nothing came of it, though they remained good friends.

Pauline attended a convent school. She grew into a tall girl, with long brown hair and a generous mouth. Her blue eyes sparkled when she smiled. Her friend Pat Cummings – a more robust girl (you had to be to take care of all those brothers) – describes Pauline as "very quiet. When she came to our house, she would ask me to walk her home if it was dusk. She was very frightened. She was not the sort to get into a car with a stranger."

Pauline and Pat were pals with Kathleen King, Kathleen Murphy, Carol Hudson, Caroline Malloy and Barbara Jepson. They played hide and seek on the crofts, or whiled away the hours by gossiping on the street corners. There was the occasional visit to the Plaza to see a new film, until the cinema was closed down and became an organ works. Pauline was always the first to go home, in the evening, because her father Amos worked at Sharples the bakery, on Cross Lane; he had to be in bed early so that he could rise early in the morning.

Pauline's reticence, however, did not prevent her from being firm when the boys got a bit out of hand – much to Paul's relief, on one occasion. He was in David Smith's bedroom, and they were wrestling on the bed. David was on top. "I looked into his face, and I thought I saw two fangs. It scared me, and I started screaming. David grabbed my throat. I hate to think what would have happened, but our Pauline shouted 'Paul' and he let me go". David's teeth seem to protrude because he has receding gums. On that occasion, however, he jammed two matchsticks in his mouth. Paul, who suffered from poor eyesight, imagined them to be the fangs of a Dracula.

* * *

The allegiances that radiated out to other groups of girls were fluid enough to keep life interesting. There was nothing like a little domestic upheaval to keep the chat going. Pat Cummings and Pauline Reade were friendly with Maureen Hindley, who was always good for a giggle. They were closer to her age group, and they had little to do with her sister Myra.

The Hindleys lived in Eaton Street, which was a continuation of Benster Street on the other side of Taylor Street. Bob Hindley, a former paratrooper, occasionally earned a few pounds by boxing in the "blood tubs", the local halls where promoters sponsored matches for modest stake money. Bob liked his share of ale, which caused friction in the household, but his wife Nellie worked hard to give her daughters a good

home. Myra was born on July 23, 1942, and Maureen followed
four years later. They were healthy girls.

The children's grandmother, Ellen Maybury, a self-effacing
little lady, lived round the corner in Bannock Street. She was
lonely, by herself, and one day the Hindleys decided that Myra
could move to her gran's. That gave the girls a bedroom each,
but it did not mean a split-up of the family. It was a two-minute
walk for Myra to get to her gran's back door. Mrs Hindley
would cook up a meal and take it round to Granny Maybury's.
Myra was constantly backward and forward between the two
houses. She still retained her duties in her parent's home. One
of them was to do her mother's hair with the curling tongs that
she heated up on the open coal fire.

Myra attended Peacock Street Primary School. She was
intelligent, but she could not override the class constraints on
her educational progress. She failed the 11-plus, and was sent
to Ryder Brow Secondary Modern School. She matured into an
attractive girl. Her high cheek bones gave her face an open look,
but a prominent parrot-like nose was the subject of occasional
hurtful comments by boys. Her nickname was Square Arse,
because of her broad 42″ hips.

Her best friend until she got married at the age of 17 was Pat
Jepson, who lived in Taylor Street. "We didn't have television
in those days. We got rid of our energy by playing a lot of
running games. It was good clean fun. I don't ever remember
Myra crying or being a bad sport."

In fact, Myra did cry once. It happened when her first close
boyfriend, Mike Higgins, drowned in a local reservoir. Pat and
Myra were 13-years-old at the time. They were due to go
swimming with the gang at the reservoir, but decided instead to
catch the No 109 bus and have tea with Pat's aunt in Reddish.
"When we got back home, we found out that Mike had
drowned. That was the only time I saw Myra cry. She started
going to church, and she took the Catholic vows. I used to go
with her to the monastery, although I was Church of England.

"Myra was a strong character. If we were going anywhere,
she picked the place to go to. We went baby-sitting together,

and she got on with kids. She was not a violent person, but if she said something, it was taken that it was done."

The two friends went through the fashions of the late '50s together. Visits to Sivori's, the Italian espresso cafe opposite the town hall in Hyde Road, for a drink of Vimto, were livened up when they started sporting tight red skirts and cardigans buttoned up at the back. Pumps were worn during the day, and high heels for the evening jive sessions at Chic Hibbert's, the rock 'n roll club at the Ashton Old Road dance hall. The new pop culture encouraged the girls to become adventurous with their hairstyles. Pat and Myra abandoned their fringes, and moved through blue and green rinses to end up as bleach blonds.

Maureen sprouted into a tall, thin girl with the same large pointed nose. Like her sister, by the time that she was chasing boys she was wearing heavy make-up and pencil-tight skirts. She sculptured the bouffant style on her head by aerosolling the walls of her heavily back-combed hair with lacquer. She chain-smoked, talked 19 to the dozen and was hyperactive. She was willing to get stuck into a fight, and proved it when she threatened to fight Maureen Siddall.

The two Maureens found they shared a common interest in David Smith. Maureen Siddall was known as The Bomber because she sported heavy leather jackets and boots. She knew David when he was just 11; she was seven years his senior, but that did not stop them from engaging in a hot affair. Their relationship cooled, however, when she visited David at the remand home and he spotted love bites on her neck. In the event, the two Maureens did not fight; instead, they became good friends.

★　★　★

Girls were always a good excuse for a fight. One memorable occasion presented itself when the Openshaw lads, whose territory was on the north side of Ashton Old Road, decided to see a film at the Essoldo. There was a fight, and Paul Cornwall, one of the Gorton boys, was given a good hiding. That, in itself, was unremarkable. What was strictly out of order was that the hiding was administered in front of his girlfriend.

The Gorton lads were playing Eddie Cochran and Duane Eddy records on the juke box in Sivori's when they heard the news. Honour had to be satisfied. Arrangements were made to call up the Deaf and Dumb boys, about eight or nine of them, from the Brook House flats in Gorton Lane. They were otherwise engaged, on this occasion, but enough support was mustered for a formidable contingent to cause havoc in Ashton Old Road during the search for the culprits.

The Openshaw lads had long ago learnt that the Gorton boys were as sharp as razors – literally. "We would go to Openshaw pubs and slip razor blades into the soap in the Gents. It might take a couple of days for the soap to wear thin, but it was not going to be a Gorton lad who had his hands cut," explains David Smith.

"Andy Capp caps were in style, for a while, and we put blades in the peaks. When the Openshaw lads tried to bait us, from the other side of Ashton Old Road, we would throw a cap. Someone would catch it and get rucked. The blades went into spuds, as well. Walking down the road, we would lob one like a grenade with those razor blades stuck in it.

"The police used to chaperone us down the street. We turned cars over in their presence, but they wouldn't dare to arrest us."

Then, Gloria Molyneux arrived. She immediately stood out from all the Gorton girls. Her long hair was naturally blond, and she spoke with a refined accent. Her father was the new caretaker at a church in Hyde Road. She was placed in St James' School, off Wellington Street. The boys made a bee-line for her, but there were only two serious contestants: Tony Latham and David Smith.

Tony had spent all his secondary school years at St James', and was acknowledged to be the cock of the school. David arrived after his expulsions from a couple of other schools, and his reputation guaranteed that there would be mutual disrespect. It did not take long for the other boys to start forming new allegiances behind Tony and David, but the question of who was the hardest of the two remained unresolved until Gloria made her appearance.

David Smith won the cupid stakes, but Gloria's father was not delighted. He visited the school one day to complain. David and Gloria were called into the headmaster's office, where Mr Molyneux "gave me a good shaking, but I wouldn't retaliate because it was the girlfriend's father. I didn't stop seeing Gloria. I stayed off school, and she came round to my house in Wiles Street."

There was an uneasy stand-off between the two rivals. They glared at each other across the playground and the football field (Tony was left-back, and David was right-back). In the end, however, the gauntlet had to be thrown down. Arrangements were made to meet for a show-down on the croft at the end of Bannock Street.

"I put it around that I had twice been to the croft, and Latham had failed to turn up," recalls Smith. Latham kept the third appointment, and was the winner. Or was he?

Latham is now reluctant to talk about those days. All that he will say is that Smith came face to face with him "and failed, terribly".

Smith puts a slightly different interpretation on the outcome. "Physically, once he got me on the floor, he beat me. But it turned out to be more of a pushing match to prove who was the strongest. If I had been on top of him, I would have made sure that I belted him. But he didn't; he just got up and walked away. If he had belted me in the face, and then turned his back on me, he would have lost; because I would have picked up a brick, and he would have been down.

"I would have been happier if we had kicked shit out of each other, because there would have been no way he would have won. I would have got him, in the end, when he was kissing his mother 'God bless'.

"But he just pinned me down. It made me feel small, but he didn't punch me. So there was no fight. Anyway, that fight didn't matter, because there was no way that he could win. If he gave me a right good pasting, I would have got all the sympathy off Gloria! What was the point of winning? I already had the prize – the girl. And it didn't improve his reputation, at school, because I was sat in the corners with Gloria Molyneux. I wasn't being one of the boys. I had 'gone soft on her'. She were great, a belting girl."

Gloria graduated before David, and moved out of the district. Tony and David kept their distance from each other, until one day Latham went down as No. 2 on Smith's murder list.

CHAPTER FOUR

Folie à Deux

1961 was a historic year. John F. Kennedy was sworn in as President of the United States, and Martin Luther King said "We shall overcome". In Britain, philosopher Bertrand Russell led a massive Trafalgar Square rally for the Campaign for Nuclear Disarmament, in which he asked: "Shall the human race survive, or shall it not?" And Prince Philip told the workers: "Gentlemen, pull your fingers out".

East-West relations were redefined. The Berlin Wall was erected, and ballet dancer Rudolph Nureyev fled from Moscow. Washington broke with Cuba, after Fidel Castro took power in Havana, and the British secret service cracked the Kroger spy ring that operated out of a bungalow in Ruislip, Middlesex.

The first American GIs were killed in Vietnam, and Yuri Gagarin beat Alan Shepherd into space.

Although she did not know it at the time, 1961 was also the year that began to shatter Myra Hindley's life. She was employed to work at Millwards Merchandising, a chemical distribution company, and found herself face-to-face with Ian Brady.

Since leaving Ryder Brow Secondary Modern, Myra had drifted aimlessly from one office job to another. For distraction, she took judo lessons, and every 10 weeks she returned to Maison Laurette in Taylor Street for a 10s 6d root toning. Her hair had been rinsed pink and blue.

Nothing had come of her engagement to Ronnie Sinclair. Although he was a low-paid tea blender at the Co-op, he managed to buy Myra a diamond ring that sported three stones, which she was pleased to show her friends in Bannock

Street. The engagement was broken off after six months, however, because Myra felt that Ronnie was too immature for her.

On January 16, 1961, at the age of 18, she reported to Millwards, to work as a shorthand typist for £8 10s a week. Ian Brady, the stock clerk who dictated her first letter, was a lanky Scotsman in a 3-piece suit. He was obviously not "one of the boys". He did play cards at lunchtime, but it became clear that he was not a good loser. Myra tried to exchange small-talk over sandwiches, but Ian was more interested in reading books by himself. He was not the gregarious sort, and he saw no point in "chatting up the birds". Betting shops had just been legalised, and he much preferred to pop out to place a cautious bet on a horse.

It was a frustrating 12 months for Myra. Restlessly, as the summer passed by, she toyed with the idea of going to work for the armed forces in Germany; she sent for the forms to join the NAAFI, the Navy, Army and Air Force Institute, but she did not return them. She had become infatuated with Ian Brady.

The progress of her romantic thoughts were chronicled in her red diary. "Ian looked at me today," was the first entry, betraying the secret yearnings of a young girl who feared that her love would go unrequited. His smiles, his failure to notice her, were all recorded. On July 23, she asked herself: "Wonder if Ian is courting".

Myra's patience was eventually rewarded. He agreed to let her eat her sandwiches with him in his tiny office in the annexe, where they could exchange the small-talk for which she now craved. Then, finally, just before Christmas 1961, she penned the words that marked success: "Eureka! Today we have our first date. We are going to the cinema".

Brady was a regular patron of the celluloid arts. He enjoyed taking photographs, but the cinema was his major interest. He particularly favoured the venue in Manchester that showed those soft porn films that were admissible on the cinema circuit. On this occasion, the film was *Trial at Nuremberg*, which was Brady's way of introducing Myra to Fascist philosophy and the

anti-semitic literature that he had begun to accumulate. On
their first date, however, Myra was more interested in her
companion than the nuances of Hitler's ideology.

* * *

Throughout 1962, Ian Brady acted out his primary fantasy. He
saw himself as a big-time villain who could make money by
robbing banks and snatching payrolls. He took Myra to see
West Side Story. They sat in the front circle of the Gaumont, and
the two-hour film about New York gangs so entranced them
that it flashed by in "what seemed like half-an-hour", recalls
Ian. Early in their relationship, however, he revealed little
about his attempts to form a gang of his own.

After his release from borstal, Ian Brady had kept in touch
with some of the inmates he met there. One of them was Philip
Deare. In July, Deare arrived in Manchester with a
hard-topped Jaguar coupé, with bucket seats. He handed it
over to another man. The car was used as a getaway vehicle.
Deare returned to his home in Bradford. On November 21 he
left home, telling his family that he was going to meet a friend.
When he arrived in Manchester, he had some bad news to
break to Ian, who had just returned from a trip to London. The
man to whom he had delivered the Jaguar had failed to
abandon the car after using it; he had held on to it for several
months, until the police arrested him. Brady was furious.

On a previous occasion, that man had failed to keep his
mouth shut after being arrested. He had informed police of the
identities of his accomplices. He knew Philip Deare's name;
and Ian Brady knew that Deare was the only route through
which the police investigation could find its way to him. Deare
was never seen again.

Brady will still not divulge the details of what he did to Philip
Deare, beyond acknowledging things like "anybody getting in
the way was dispensable", a spine-chilling statement which we
now know has to be treated seriously.

When I pressed him for information about the youth's death,

he suggested: "It was an accident. I don't know whether the death . . . "

Here, his voice trailed away. "I can't touch it because it's like a thread on a jumper. Once it starts, the whole thing begins to unravel."

But on one point he was insistent. "Deare is not connected in any way with the, shall we say, rotten branch that grew out after I met Myra. At least it had nothing to do with the Moors. They can't bring that into the Moors, not that lad Deare."

Even Myra had not yet learnt the sinister significance of the moors to Ian Brady. But 22 years later she vividly recalled what happened soon after Ian's last meeting with Philip Deare.[1] Ian announced one Saturday that they were going to ride on his motorbike up to Bradford. When they arrived, Ian "told me to go to this house and ask for this boy Deare.

"I knocked on the door and the boy's dad answered. He said they hadn't seen him for a while, and that he was probably in his sister's house.

"When I got back and told Ian, he insisted that I go to the sister's house and ask for him, which I did.

"The sister also said she had not seen him for some time. I told her I was an ex-girlfriend, and when she saw him would she give him my address and ask him to call.

"Two weeks later a letter came. I knew it was concerning this episode, so I steamed the letter open although it was addressed to me. All it said was that he had still not shown up, and when he did they would let me know.

"I re-sealed the letter, and that night we went to the cinema. I gave him the letter, and he went to the toilet. He came back really furious. He asked if I had read the letter. I admitted that I had, and he didn't talk to me for a week.

"I think, now, that he had already murdered that boy, and he just wanted to know the family's reaction".

---

[1] Unless otherwise attributed, the statements by Myra Hindley which are quoted in this chapter were made to Rena Duffy, a friend, in Cookham Wood Prison, Kent, between June 30 and July 4, 1985.

This is the first known occasion on which Ian Brady revealed his morbid curiosity about the family of one of his victims.

* * *

In the eyes of the naive girl from Gorton, Ian Brady was a charismatic figure. He was tall, and handsome, and she liked the way he pushed his brown hair into place by raking his fingers through the thick mop on his head.

Ian Brady had a style that set him apart from the uncouth youths with whom Myra had been reared in Taylor Street. He took fastidious care with his clothes. His grey suits had to be made of cloth that was the correct mixture of Terylene and wool. The turn-ups on his trousers were regarded as the mark of an old man's style, in those days of the mini-skirt and Carnaby Street fashions. To Myra Hindley, however, they became the sign of good taste. Ian did not buy his clothes off the peg; he invited a Jewish tailor round to his home to measure him up.

He was generous with his money. He escorted Myra to restaurants for oriental meals, and he insisted on drinking German wines. His opinionated conversation with "the girl" – as Ian often referred to her – was deemed to be the sign of education.

His visits to Granny Maybury's house became increasingly frequent during 1962. Dressed in a long trenchcoat, leather headware and goggles, he cut a dashing figure on his motorcycle. Weekend trips to the countryside were delightful interludes. Wine was drunk from the bottle after it had been chilled in a mountain stream. When they stopped at a pub, Ian checked to make sure that it was a country inn with genuine old oak beams – not the imitation kind with thick black glossy paint to conceal the age of the timber. And he took a special delight in examining the old copper and brass ornaments displayed on the walls.

The glacial look in Ian's eyes betrayed a hard heart that by now knew no compassion for other human beings. To Myra, however, that penetrating gaze sent a chill of excitement down her spine. She was yet to discover that the man whom she took as her lover was a psychopath, a man who killed either to protect himself or because it gave him a deep sense of relief from the stress that kept building up inside him.

He was now well advanced in developing the detail of a philosophy to match the granite in his soul. In 1959, he had begun to accumulate tape recordings of Nuremberg speeches by Adolph Hitler. He listened to them time and again, and he was thrilled to discover anew what he regarded as the relevance of fascism to world history.

Towards Myra, however, Ian was attentive and kind. On New Year's eve, when she took him to her parent's home in Eaton Street – his contribution to the celebrations was a bottle of whisky – he was the model of charm. "Dad and Ian spoke as if they'd known each other for years. Ian is so gentle he makes me want to cry," she recorded in her diary.

Without realising it, however, Myra's character was slowly undergoing a metamorphosis under the spell of Ian's poisoned mind. Week in, week out, at their lunchtime tête-à-tête, on their way to the cinema, in the privacy of Granny Maybury's front room, he introduced her to his outlook on life.

He encouraged her to read books such as *Mein Kampf*, *Six Million Dead*, and *Eichmann*, which they borrowed from the local public libraries. They became familiar figures to Barbara Hughes, who had just begun her career as a trainee librarian. In fact, she frequently saw Myra Hindley in Mount Road, while queueing for her bus on her way to the Levenshulme branch. Myra passed the spot on her way to Millwards. "She wore quite short skirts, even before the mini-skirt was in fashion, so the first impression was that she was tarty, a bit common. That's why I thought they were not suited.

"When he returned his books at the Longsight branch, he never said 'Please' or 'Thank you'. He always walked straight to the True Crime shelves, crash hat under his arm. They frequently came into Levenshulme library, chatting together, but they never spoke to the staff."

Myra absorbed Ian's attitudes as he callously dehumanised

people in his everyday speech, calling them insects, morons and maggots. She was fascinated as he discoursed on ethnic minorities, particularly the Jews and the blacks, and she was entranced by what she thought were his penetrating arguments against organised religion. In this way, he substituted a crazy hotch-potch of evil ideas in place of the workaday attitudes on which Myra had been weaned in Gorton.

Maureen began to notice the changes. They were small things, at first, but they accumulated into a clear transformation of her sister's character. As a teenager, Myra enjoyed playing with the children and babies whom she looked after for pocket money; now she disliked babies. Her religious values were abandoned in favour of the banal arguments of the atheist. Marriage became an anachronistic institution to be despised, and social occasions, such as dances, were avoided in preference for her secretive sojourns with Ian Brady.

Myra became the victim of a condition known to psychiatrists as *Folie à Deux*. She came to share Ian's insanity. Her character was adapted to blend with his. This is how the condition is described in one leading text book:

"While they are conceived in isolation, paranoid reactions show a particular tendency to spread by psychological contagion. In the narrow circle of the family this tendency may be the cause of *Folie à Deux*, as when a husband takes on and believes the delusions of his paranoid wife. In such circumstances one usually finds that one member of the pair or more of affected persons is suffering from an organic or endogenous illness, while the others are ill only in a social sense".[2]

Myra Hindley was now as ill as her psychopathic lover, Ian Brady.

* * *

It was one thing to colour someone's attitudes, quite another to inveigle that person into murder. Ian Brady knew that, if he

[2] Eliot Slater and Martin Roth, *Clinical Psychiatry*, 3rd edn., London: Baillière Tindall, 1977, p. 149.

was to establish a lasting relationship with Myra, she would sooner or later learn his darkest secret: that, out of psychological necessity, he had killed, and would continue to kill. He could not, however, bluntly invite her to join him in one of his homicidal outings without carefully preparing her for the ultimate crime: the perfect murder.

Early in 1963 he began to introduce her to the idea that the two of them could make money by robbing a bank or a store. Her initial reaction to the proposition is unknown; but we do know that at some early stage, she agreed to go along with the idea. There were practical problems, the principal one of which was that they could not make their get-away astride a small motorcycle. They needed a car, and Myra agreed to qualify as a driver.

During the course of the year, she failed her test three times. That did not deter Ian from elaborating on the fantasy that they would proceed with the arrangements. He even committed those arrangements to paper, when he wrote to her on April 16, 1963, to explain that a sprained ankle had prevented him from reporting for work.

In his letter, he discussed the prospect of buying a car from a local used-car dealer. But he went further, and suggested that he would "capitalise" on the fact that he could not go to work. "I shall grasp this opportunity to view the investment establishment situated in Stockport Road, next Friday, to go over details."

In the clumsy code that he used extensively in his notes in the coming three years, he informed Myra that he would conduct a surveillance operation on a bank, to work out the best time to attempt a robbery.

Myra was a willing partner in this charade. She bought an Austin mini-van, which immediately liberated the lovers. From the public scrutiny on the exposed back of a motor-cycle, they were now able to ensconce themselves in the privacy of the tiny vehicle. Although she was not legally entitled to drive the van without the company of a qualified driver, Myra did so without being caught. She began calling for Ian to take him to work; but following his instructions, she did not knock on the door of his mother's home in Westmorland Street. She waited for him at the end of the road.

In June, Maureen, now aged 17, also secured a job at Millwards. She was made to promise that she would not tell the other employees that Ian and Myra were secretly building up a close association. In that same month, Ian moved in to Bannock Street with Myra and her grandmother. He had finally committed himself to a life-long relationship.

But he could not bring himself to say: "I love you". That did not worry Myra unduly, because she had monitored the small signs that told her what she needed to know. On one occasion, when they were sitting at one end of a long table in a pub, a group of men arrived and sat at the other end. They took an exaggerated interest in the blond, and "Ian started shouting and offering to take them all on. I was secretly pleased".

Neither sex nor a time-honoured social convention like marriage was sufficient for their unique relationship. He had to prove his fidelity in his own way, so that Myra would be left in no doubt about his devotion to her. He had to execute an act of such supreme finality that it would bind them together for eternity.

PART TWO

Consecration

CHAPTER FIVE

The Dance

Amos Reade arrived home from the bakery early in the afternoon. He had a nap, and then strolled across to the Steel Works, his weekday pub on the corner of Gorton Lane and Preston Street, for his early evening pint of ale. He was back home in Wiles Street for his tea – tailend of silver hake, chips and peas – at 7.30 p.m. It was Friday, July 12, 1963.

His wife Joan was flustered.

"Your tea's not ready, Amos," said Mrs Reade as her husband stepped from the cobbled street into the front room. "I'm trying to find someone to go to the dance with our Pauline."

Amos Reade settled into his armchair with the newspaper. The minutes ticked by.

Pauline came downstairs and glanced at her father.

"You do look pretty," he told her. Amos was proud of his daughter.

The compliment escaped Pauline; she was more concerned about whether her parents would stop her from going to the dance.

She had tried to find a friend to go with her. On the way home from work at the confectioners, she had called on Linda Bradshaw, but her mother had put her foot down firmly: Linda was not going to a dance where alcohol was on sale.

Then she called in at Pat Garvey's, around the corner in Benster Street. The two of them had bought similar white pleated skirts at C & A's, which they wore for the first time at the dance the previous Friday.

"Are you still coming to the club tonight?" asked Pauline.

"No," replied Pat. "Me mum won't let me. She found out they sell booze there."

So Pauline went home to get ready. She slipped into her pink dress, the one with the square neck, brushed back her black hair and waited for her dad.

Amos Reade was not worried. Pauline was sixteen years old, a sensible girl, and the dance was only up the road in Chapman Street.

"I'll get your tea, dad," said Pauline.

But Mr Reade knew his daughter had other things on her mind, that evening, and he was not going to hold her up. "Your mother will do it," he said.

Pauline picked up her powder blue coat and white gloves. "I'll go and see if Barbara can come with me," she called as she disappeared out of the front door. It was 7.45 p.m.

Mrs Reade rushed the fish onto a plate and five minutes later caught up with Pauline in Taylor Street.

Barbara Jepson could not go to the dance either, so Mrs Reade decided to have a word with Linda Bradshaw's mother. They walked quickly round to her home in Bannock Street. Pauline waited in the street, playing with the Bradshaw twins in their pram, while her mother went in. No good: Mrs Bradshaw would not relent. Her Linda was not going to the working men's club where they sold beer.

"I'll just have to go on my own," said Pauline, and she turned and walked away from her mother down Taylor Street. It was a few minutes past 8 p.m.

Pauline turned right into Eaton Street, crossed the road opposite the Hindley home, and cut through the backyard of the Shakespeare pub – "the Shaky" to the residents of the Taylor Street area – and into Gorton Lane. Her mother never saw her again.

* * *

Pat Cummings, who was a year younger than Pauline, did not believe that her shy friend would dare go to the dance on her own. That is what she had predicted when she was talking about it earlier in the day with Dorothy Slater. They decided to wait on the croft at the back of Benster Street, to see if Pauline went by. She did, about 8 pm.

The two girls followed Pauline as she walked up Gorton Lane. The Beyer Peacock works were on their left. Nearly 6,000 steam locomotives had been built on the other side of that wall over the previous 100 years. Richard Peacock established the company in 1855, and in doing so he did more to transform Gorton's agricultural base than anyone else. It was the rock-solid foundation for the local economy which, alas, with the nationwide electrification of the railways, was causing severe financial problems for the company.

Pat and Dorothy watched Pauline turn into Froxmer Street. She was about 100 yards ahead of them.

Beyer Peacock's 20-foot high wall blots out the west side of Froxmer Street. On the east side were a few rows of houses separated by a croft.

Pauline walked north towards Railway Street, and was almost at the end of Froxmer Street when Pat and Dorothy turned off it to cut across the croft. This was the short cut which would bring them out at the top end of Railway Street, where they planned to watch Pauline walk by them. To get to the dance, Pauline had to walk the length of Railway Street, turn left, cross the railway bridge and complete the short walk to the workingmen's club, just one mile from the front door of her home.

Pat and Dorothy waited on in Railway Street, but Pauline did not emerge from Froxmer Street. After a short while, they retraced their steps, but there was no sign of Pauline. She had vanished.

Mrs Reade, meanwhile, was back in her home by 8.15 p.m. Amos had finished his tea and she cleaned up. She was troubled. She did not like Pauline going out by herself, but you have to cut the apron strings sometime.

It was a warm summer's evening. She fussed around the house and about 9.15 p.m. she opened the door to let in some fresh air. Paul would be coming home soon. As she swung the door open, she spotted something white in the road.

Three short steps took her across the flagstone pavement. She stooped and picked up one of Pauline's white gloves. She must have dropped it as she went out. Mrs Reade tucked the glove into the drawer of the sideboard in the kitchen, and went to bed. She was not feeling well.

★   ★   ★

Paul, a year younger than his sister, hurried back from the cinema. He turned off Taylor Street into Benster Street and paused to watch the excitement. David Smith was slapping his girlfriend Maureen Hindley about the face.

The pair of them stood in Charmers Street, at the top end of the entry behind Wiles Street. Their voices were raised. Maureen called for help. Myra was standing on the opposite corner, looking at them.

Paul, like the other youths in the neighbourhood, had learnt to treat David Smith with the respect that is born of fear.

But the anxiety went deeper than that for Paul Reade. He regarded David as a bit weird. On a number of occasions, when playing in No 13, Smith had flicked on his tape-recorder to grind out strange sounds – Paul didn't like to call it music. "David used to call up the Devil," recalls Paul. "He would tap the cast-iron fire with a poker and say 'There it is, it's coming now, now watch carefully', and then he would say 'It's here'. It was spooky. I would turn round and say 'Get lost, David', and on one occasion he threw the poker at me and it hit me on the back of the head." Paul Reade was short-sighted, and not the brightest of lads; tailor-made for someone who wanted to shock with a macabre game.

There was no way in which Paul Reade was going to stop David Smith from giving Maureen Hindley a good hiding. He crossed the road and walked past Myra. She was one of his childhood friends with whom he used to play games on the crofts, but he was late for his tea and was not going to intervene. As he turned into Wiles Street, he looked back. Maureen was still crying. Myra walked across and split them up.

Paul hurried down the cul-de-sac. As he reached his house, he glanced at David Smith's front door. No. 13 was open. But then, it was a warm night and not unusual for folk to leave their doors ajar. Paul stepped off the pavement and into his living room. It was 9.30 pm.

At 2 a.m., Mr and Mrs Reade got dressed and scoured the dark streets for Pauline. The frantic search continued into the next day.

Mrs Reade saw Linda Leadbeater at the No. 109 bus stop opposite the Steel Works. "Have you seen Pauline?" "No, Mrs Reade."

The tears had left channel marks through the powder on Mrs Reade's cheeks. Her long black hair, usually well groomed, was dishevelled, and her heart was beating rapidly.

"If you had gone to the dance last night, our Pauline would have come home," said Mrs Reade, levelling her awesome accusation at Linda. The girl turned and ran home. But Mrs Leadbeater told her not to worry: Pauline would eventually return.

The police searched the fairground caravans on the rec. in Casson Street. It did not take long for the rumour to get around that Pauline was pregnant and had run away with one of the fairground boys. According to another story which quickly began to circulate, Pauline, who had gone to the dance with 10s in her pocket, had gone to live in Australia.

An uneasiness descended on the Taylor Street community. Children do not just disappear – not when you have known them from when they were babies. You can cope with it, when one of them dies. There is a period of mourning, and then the grief dissolves into a private loss for the family. But, no-one can escape the anxiety that courses through the streets when one of the neighbour's children disappears into the night.

Myra Hindley was infected by that collective panic when Maureen disappeared one night. She drove round to Pat

Jepson's house. Her boyfriend, Ian, waited in the van while she went indoors to talk to Pat. "Have you seen our Maureen? She's gone missing."

Pat had not seen Maureen for several weeks. "Myra was really worried," she recalls. "Pauline had just gone missing."

CHAPTER SIX

The Death

From Market Harborough, it is a short drive north along the A6 to Gallow Fields Road. On the left, its towers and high walls dimly visible through the mist, is one of Britain's maximum security prisons. The approach road to Gartree offers no shelter for escapees: it is devoid of hedges and trees. The ploughed field is flat and expansive, which is why the RAF used it as an aerodrome in World War II.

There is not much chance of escape from Gartree. Even the tops of the walls are tubular-shaped, offering no anchorage for a grappling iron.

It was November 29, 1984, and I was on my way to see Ian Brady. The prison officer took my visiting order, checked it against his records, and examined my passport photograph in his file. Ian Brady's Category A status meant that his visitors had to be vetted. Not that he had many people to tea. Apart from Lord Longford, I was the first person he had agreed to see in nine years.

I wanted the answers to so many questions which, in the end, would help me to understand Brady and Hindley. There were still too many untidy strands left in the case. We still did not know for sure who was their first victim. The answer to that question, I felt sure, would reveal a great deal about the nature of their relationship. Pauline Reade was the obvious candidate, because she died a month after Brady had set up home with Myra. But their guilt was still supposition, and there were some obvious reasons for thinking that Pauline was not murdered by them: she was one of Maureen's friends, and she lived too close to Brady's new home for comfort. But until Pauline's death was solved, the doubts would inevitably linger on.

I knew I was not going to be able to tick off the answers against a neat list of questions. The secrets were buried in a deeply troubled mind, and I would have to be patient while Ian Brady got the measure of me.

Families congregated in the annexe. One by one, they were called into the large visiting room. They gathered around the tables that were lined up in rows, and waited for the first glimpse of the convict with whom they had come to spend two hours, a snatch in time which provided the memories that relieved the endless stream of tedium as a guest of Her Majesty.

I was left alone, until special arrangements were made for an officer to act as my escort. He took me through two gates on the outer wall and into a courtyard that led to the inner fence. "Mr Harrison to see Brady," said the officer into the inter-com. By remote control, the gate was unlocked, and we passed through into the heart of the prison. A 50-yard walk took us to the hospital wing, a ground floor building that had one permanent inmate: Ian Brady. The notorious reputation of the child killer meant that he could not be housed in one of the blocks. That would expose him to the private vengeance of the other prisoners.

We talked desultorily about the inmates as we approached the hospital. A jangle of keys, and the officer opened the door. "This one's given up," he said. He was preparing me for the shock of my first meeting with Ian Brady. I was shown into the dentist's surgery, which was to serve as the visiting room. The officer collected a chair from another room, placed it strategically in the corridor so that he could see into the surgery, and relaxed for the afternoon.

It *was* a shock. Ian Brady looked like an old man of 70. He was stoop-shouldered, his cheeks were shrunken, and his clothes were draped on skin and bone. The hand I shook was devoid of flesh, turning the long fingers into talons. His hair still retained some of its vigour of youth, but otherwise there was no sign of life in the man.

Ian Brady survived on his hatred for the officials of the Home Office, whom he was convinced were trying to destroy him.

Their treatment of him, he said, was malignant. "I would prefer to be a tramp in India than in a prison in England," he said. "I would rather float down the Ganges without a paddle and face the crocodiles – at least I would have a chance of getting to the bank."

I broke open the blue packet of Gauloise cigarettes. Ian had given me strict instructions on what to bring: the heavy-duty, untipped kind. Lord Longford usually forgot to get the right brand, which served as a cause of irritation. Brady drew deeply on his first cigarette. Then we chain-smoked in a conspiracy against the system. I was not allowed to take him tobacco, but he could smuggle the dog-ends back into his cell. The more we smoked in two hours, the bigger the booty that he could take back with him, to roll and savour and thereby relieve the tension of the night.

Brady's hatred for authority quickly surfaced. The IRA had recently planted a bomb in a hotel in Brighton, in an attempt to wipe out the British Cabinet. The Prime Minister, Margaret Thatcher, escaped with her life, but one of her Ministers, Norman Tebbit, was seriously injured. Four members of the Conservative Party died. What did Ian think of the attempted assassination? "Quite honestly, I wish it had been a 200 lb bomb instead of a 20 lb bomb. Thatcher, Tebbit and Keith Joseph – they should all have been buried. I am not speaking for myself, but for the country. There is no end to the damage they are doing."

Brady did not think that his callous attitude was exceptional. People were generally capable of killing, he insisted. "What about Hitler? People say that if they could foresee the future, they would kill."

But there were more cheerful moments in our conversation. Brady is locked in a time warp, his mind filled with the ideas and images of the early 1960s when he roamed the countryside with Myra Hindley. He reminisced about the clear water and the fish in the brooks by the road to Glasgow. As they cruised along the winding lanes, they listened to Radio Caroline, the pirate station anchored three miles off the coast, in the North

Sea. "I used to say 'Let's go back another time'. There are many 'other times' that I have missed."

I wanted to talk about Pauline Reade and Keith Bennett, but he wanted to recall his childhood trips in Scotland. They caught the steamer at Oban, and sailed to Tobermory. The island was enchanting. They stayed on a farm, which was surrounded by purple heather and wild deer.

Why did he adamantly refuse to cooperate with the Parole Board, which had a duty to consider the future of all prisoners? Not because he did not like the idea of freedom; far from it. But he would not be allowed to enjoy freedom in Britain, where the public's attention would severely restrict him. No, but he would love to live in France. He would occupy a peasant's farmhouse, and roam the country lanes. But it was a dream, because even if he was granted parole he would not be given permission to leave Britain.

And so he made the best of the idea of freedom in his cell. He fed the birds outside his window. But he had long since given up exercise. That was restricted to opening his window, and letting in the fresh air. But the air around Gartree, which was built near a marsh, was not particularly pleasant to Ian Brady. The mists sweep in at night, and "I expect a 1930s Dracula to come out of the dark".

John the orderly knocked at the door. Tea? Brady's plastic mug was handed in, the liquid black and sweet. It was 4.10 p.m., and the guard in the corridor was getting restless. It was time to go. Brady stood up and took my hand. "I enjoyed myself, and I feel strong," he said. There was the barest flicker of a smile on his gaunt face, and he was gone.

* * *

For 19 years Ian Brady maintained a stoic silence about the disappearance of Pauline Reade. He was equally silent about 12-year-old Keith Bennett, a blue-eyed boy with fair hair and poor eye-sight who vanished a year after Pauline, on June 18, 1964, while walking down Stockport Road, Longsight. Keith was on his way to his grandmother's house, a half-mile walk from his home, where he was going to spend the night.

These two cases remained open in the files at Manchester police headquarters, and senior detectives visited Brady on several occasions over the years in the forlorn hope of learning something about their fate. At no stage did he acknowledge any connection with their disappearances. Would he be equally uncooperative with me?

My second visit to Gartree was on January 21, 1985. Luck was on my side: the jailers allowed me to spend the two hours in the privacy of Cell 4. The heavy metal door was swung open, and I was confronted by the Moors murderer in his lair. Ian was sitting in his armchair, typing on his braille machine. He was transcribing a book about the highland clearances that had been sent to him by a school for blind children in Liverpool. His work for the blind was his one – private – act of atonement for his crimes. He dismissed with contempt the idea of making a public declaration of his remorse.

A chair was pushed through the door, and I sat down in front of Ian Brady. He sat upright in his armchair, his back to the window. His face was unshaven, which accentuated his haggard appearance. He wore blue denim trousers, the legs of which hung loosely over his bony knees, and a blue jumper, the holes in which had been crudely darned.

On his left was his bed, the blanket tucked tightly under the mattress. On the bed was his braille machine and the tobacco which he used to roll his cigarettes. On his right was a ledge on which he made sweets with condensed milk and icing sugar. A bowl of custard stood on the ledge outside his window: he put it there to go cold and lumpy, which was the way he liked to eat it.

It was a good meeting. We discoursed at length on Dostoyevsky, and on Myra's renewed campaign for parole. The conversation turned to guilt, and he accepted that his was a criminal guilt, the responsibility for which he did not seek to evade – unlike "those people who killed thousands of people by dropping bombs on Dresden", and who then salved their consciences by throwing responsibility on to the State.

Our tea arrived, and time was moving on. I wanted to bring
Ian up to date with the news, so I handed him a cutting from
the previous day's *Mail on Sunday*, in which columnist Alan
Williams referred to Myra's quest for parole. Williams was not
sympathetic, and he used the opportunity for some fresh
Longford baiting. "Perhaps before he makes any further move
in his campaign to get Myra Hindley released, Lord Longford
might persuade this evil woman to put the minds of the Reade
and Bennett families finally at rest," wrote Williams.

Brady glanced at the cutting, and placed it slowly on his bed.
He was sceptical about the intentions of the Parole Board,
which had just begun the process of reviewing their cases.[1]
Ought Myra to be released? Slowly, painfully, Ian Brady
wrenched the words from his tortured mind. He said that if he
"expanded" on the events that had occurred during their mad
years together, "she would never get out in 100 years".

The light was fading outside, and Cell 4 was almost dark. Ian
was silhouetted against the window, but I could see that his lips
were pursed as he struggled with words of pain. There was a
deathly silence. I held my breath lest I make a noise that would
break the spell. It was the closest that Ian Brady had come to
admitting that other things had happened for which they had
not yet been brought to account. What did he mean?

He raised a bony finger, and pointed at the newspaper
cutting. "Things like that."

This was the first time in 20 years that Ian Brady accepted
that he at least knew something about the disappearance of
Pauline Reade and Keith Bennett. Twenty years of silence were
broken with three little words: not enough to constitute a
confession that would convince a court of law, although enough
to satisfy me. But there was more.

[1] Brady's cynicism was warranted. When the Home Secretary, Leon
Brittan, finally announced his decision on May 23, 1985, he coupled
his rejection of Hindley's request for parole with a decision not to
review her case again for a further five years. She regarded this as an
infringement of her human rights, and she instructed her solicitors to
appeal to the European Court of Justice in Strasburg.

David Smith, he said, the man who had "shopped" him for the killing of 17-year-old Edward Evans, was deeply implicated in the evil that he had created with Myra Hindley. Smith "has more blood on him than I do". Smith and his wife, Maureen – but she was dead, now, said Brady, so she did not matter.

It was 4 p.m., and time was running out. Would Brady ever return to the subject in the future, when there was more time for him to elaborate on his allegations? For two decades the public had assumed that David Smith was just a young dupe who got out of his depth when Brady butchered the Evans boy. What was the truth? The questions welled up inside me, but the officer in the corridor was getting fidgety. 4.15 p.m.: time to go.

The nagging doubts surfaced as I drove south to London on the M1. First, Brady had not accepted direct responsibility for killing Pauline Reade and Keith Bennett. Second, he might be using the smear technique to finally retaliate against the man who put him behind bars for life. Was he lying? Were his words the wild ramblings of a demented mind, or was a murderer walking free? Was Brady prodding me into a search for the truth, or was he trying to use me as his instrument of revenge?

* * *

I was due to fly to San Diego in February, to attend a conference on nuclear disarmament, so I deferred my next visit to Ian Brady until March 12. At the entrance to the prison, I handed in a Made in Korea radio. The officer logged the gifts which visitors were taking in. The radio was checked to make sure that it met the regulatory specifications: no mains connection, and no VHF or FM wavebands. Ian's set was on the blink, and he had expressed the wish for a replacement. He particularly wanted a Grundig-made Concert Boy, but I was not able to find one in the shops.

He was waiting for me in his cell. Into his stomach he was cradling a white plastic orange juice container, which he used as a hot water bottle. Gently, I brought him back to the sensitive subject. Why, I asked, did Smith tell the police about the murder of Edward Evans?

"Well, it was his nerves."

What of the other killings? Was Smith involved in them?

BRADY I mean, the one that they keep on about, lived two doors down from him. That's one of them.

HARRISON She was one of them, was she?

BRADY [nodding his head affirmatively] Hmm.

HARRISON But it still doesn't explain, I mean he could have protected himself completely if he'd made a clean breast of everything. He would have got off Scott free.

BRADY Well, the police were after him.

HARRISON Pardon?

BRADY The police were after him. They can't prove it now because his house is demolished.

HARRISON What happened?

BRADY I don't want to go into stuff like that, you know, it's . . .

This was hardly the evidence on which to accuse a man of being an accessory to murder. David Smith, whatever he had done before October 6, 1965, redeemed himself that day when he telephoned the police and brought to an end the wilful slaughter of children. Even so, there were two mothers in Manchester who wanted to know what had happened to their children.

We returned to Pauline Reade on April 3. I suggested that Smith could not have been involved in their early murders, which meant that he was not implicated in Pauline's death.

BRADY He was next door to one which the police were interested in.

HARRISON One that they never got you on?

BRADY Yeh, they questioned me on it, and he [Smith] was next door, and his wife had dresses, dresses belonging to this one.

HARRISON   What are you saying, that he did it?

BRADY   I'm saying that . . . I can't . . . that one [Pauline Reade] I'm involved, she [Myra] is involved of course. The other one [Maureen] is dead, now, so it doesn't matter. I can't go into the details of that one.

Brady wanted to break off the discussion about Pauline, except to insist that her death did not occur in the house that he occupied in Bannock Street with Myra. "Not my house, another one, not my house."

★   ★   ★

Ian Brady was now becoming anxious about my persistent interest in Pauline Reade. I arrived on April 23 for another session, and he quickly raised the issue.

BRADY   I gave you more information.

HARRISON   What, you mean about him [Smith] having her clothes and things?

BRADY   Yeh.

HARRISON   Do you really think that he was that involved, there, because that was very early on, wasn't it?

BRADY   I can't really say. It involves me, umm, I just can't remember, I can't be done now, his house is demolished.

HARRISON   His house?

BRADY   Yeh.

HARRISON   What was in it? You did mention that it contained something or other, you didn't say what it was, though.

Ian Brady was silent for about 15 seconds, an eternity for an inquisitor who thinks that he may at last be on the verge of discovering the truth about one of the worst crimes in modern British criminal history. The memories were crashing through what Ian Brady calls the "blocks" in his mind, torturing him with the pain that I saw through the slits in his eyes. He leaned his head forward slowly. There was a conflict that had to be resolved in his mind: whether to talk or not. The strain showed on every muscle in his face. He pursed his lips, and the few remaining words came out with a hiss.

BRADY Blood.

HARRISON Yeh, in his house, so the kid died in his house, did she?

BRADY Well, see, I can't go into the details. Otherwise, the whole thing will come out untimely, you know.

HARRISON Yes, but of course, people keep putting all the blame on you, don't they?

BRADY Oh, I know that, know that, but I'm not opting out, I'm not opting out. We used the axe on Evans . . .

The blocks came down, and he was exhausted. Both physically and psychologically, Ian Brady was a broken man. Pity was out of place, and he did not seek it. But was his allegation against Myra Hindley and David Smith – that they had both conspired with him to kill Pauline Reade in No 13 Wiles Street, two doors from her own home – the fantasy of a demented mind? Perhaps so, but he had uttered the words, and I was now charged with the responsibility of establishing the truth. That much I owed to Amos and Joan Reade.

CHAPTER SEVEN

Myra's Curse

Ian Brady's psychological condition began to deteriorate rapidly during June 1985. He spelt out his plan to kill a warder if – as he expected – he failed to get the civil courts to uphold his complaint that he was being maltreated. "I'm going to lose anyway, so I may as well get some personal satisfaction." That, he explained, meant killing someone "on the way down. That's the quickest way to do it." Killing "is a squaring up. I think they have taken enough fucking pounds off me, in the Shylock sense." They had turned him into a coat-hanger, he said. "They want me dead. Take somebody with me, I don't see winning it at any level, you see."

He was determined to go to court to prove a point. "I want people to see an example of what 20 years of an enlightened, modern penal system produced – fuck all. They don't neglect me, as far as harrassment and goading me is concerned. They treat me like a monkey in a cage – they keep poking me with a stick. The monkey might not react for days, but when it does react, they say 'Ah, I told you so'. That's the position I'm in. No matter how much positive effort I make, they want that label [the Moors Murderer] stuck, because it's a question of 'isolate, store, destroy'."

I returned to Gartree seven days later, but there was no improvement. Ian was in an angry mood, his speech almost incomprehensible. His repeated requests for a transfer to a mental hospital had come to nothing, and he felt that his few friends and confidants were dragging their heels – even conspiring against him behind his back.

In fact, Lord Longford had arranged for Brady to be examined by Dr John McCulloch, the Medical Director of Park

Lane Hospital, Liverpool. A transfer could only be achieved if the Home Office was convinced by its own psychiatrists that he really was in need of treatment.

Brady's solicitor, Benedict Birnberg, had been instructed to serve a High Court writ against the Home Office, claiming damages for allegedly neglecting to provide him with appropriate psychiatric treatment. This, it was hoped, would provide extra pressure on the Home Office. Shrewdly, Mr Birnberg made a tactical decision not to serve the writ until the McCulloch report was on the Home Secretary's desk and available as part of the evidence in any court proceedings.

I pointed this out to Ian as we sat in the dentist's room. It was my eighth visit to Gartree. I was also feeling angry. Intuitively, I felt that Ian had lied to me about David Smith's involvement in the Pauline Reade murder, and that this was a betrayal of the trust that had built up between us. When I challenged Ian, he became even more furious: he half rose from his chair, his face strained fearsomely, and his hands rose to clutch the air in frustration. Was I also against him, that I could not accept his word?

I managed to calm him down. Even as a layman, I could see that Ian was in an extremely bad state. His night-time hallucinations were intensifying. He complained that the "blocks" in his mind were slipping more frequently, now; that he was not able to fend off the voices, which kept asking him questions about his other murders. The Home Office "scum" obviously wanted him dead; that was why they were piping the "garbage" through the central heating system at night, to disturb his sleep and disorientate him. He had more chance of living if he were riding down the Ganges on the back of a crocodile.

It was his threat to kill a warder that finally persuaded me that I had to intervene in some positive way. We were talking about the Mental Health Act which governed the transfer of prisoners to places like Broadmoor, the top security mental hospital. The regulations had been amended since the last time a psychiatrist had recommended that he was a suitable case for treatment. Ian became despondent and said that, if he was turned down again, he had one remedy left: he would kill an officer, and then commit suicide. He had no doubt that he could succeed. They were used to seeing a weak, broken old man sloping around the corridor between his cell and the latrine, and they had dropped their guard. When the time was right, he would pounce. What could I do, I asked him? Lord Longford had his platform: the benches of the House of Lords. And Mr Birnberg could use the courts to press his case. I wanted to write a book, but that would take some time to prepare. There was only one avenue immediately open to me. I was the *Sunday People's* chief reporter, and I knew that my newspaper would publish my articles. Ian agreed that I should proceed, if that would advance his chances of receiving psychiatric treatment.

We shook hands, and I left. As I drove back to London, I wrestled with a dilemma. There was no difficulty in reporting the facts about his physical condition. He was now down to below 8 stone, an alarming loss of weight that was due to his psychosomatic condition. But what about his confession that he and Myra – and David Smith – had killed Pauline Reade? He would not have expected me to report his admissions.

The accusation against Smith was a libellous one, which I knew we could not defend in court; that would have to be omitted from my story. But should I accept any additional self-censorship? Brady might have wished me to do so: but he had already gone on record as condemning "such anachronisms as censors",[1] and I decided to take his strictures to heart. My first article, on June 23, was launched with the screaming banner headline: MY SECRET MURDERS.

* * *

Myra Hindley was horrified when she heard the news. She was in her first floor cell in the south wing of Cookham Wood Prison, Kent. The pink floral curtains and plants in a basket

[1] Frank Longford, *The Grain of Wheat*, London: Collins, 1974, p. 147.

gave the room a cheerfulness which suddenly evaporated when she heard the radio broadcast. The announcer reported that Ian Brady had confessed that he and Myra Hindley had killed two other children. Myra was dumb-struck.

That kind of publicity would not help her campaign for parole. Just a few weeks previously, she had appealed for help to the European Court of Justice. Her mentor, Lord Longford, tried to limit the damage by pointing out that Ian Brady was not a reliable witness, which cast doubt on his confession. He declared in an interview:

"He is mental. I don't like to say that about anyone, a fellow human being, but he's a very disturbed person. He always has been. The state of his mind is so volatile, it's very hard to know whether to take that sort of thing seriously or not.

"I've seen him since those stories began coming out and I asked what he felt about them. And he said: 'Not authorised, but no other comment'. In other words he doesn't say he repudiates them, he doesn't say he agrees with them. He's quite shrewd in his own rather dotty way."[2]

Myra was more forthright in her attack. She claimed that Brady's confession was a fabrication. Her statement was published on August 4:

"Ever since I broke off contact with Ian Brady 13 years ago, he has been implying that he could implicate me in 'other matters.' I have always denied this. If he does have information about other killings then I wish he would tell what he knows to the police – and not just to journalists and psychiatrists – to end the speculation."[3]

Myra was calling her former lover's bluff. Was she innocent, or was she playing a dangerous game? Had Brady used me in a private vendetta against Myra, or was he really trying to expunge the guilt in his soul with the truth?

It was my second article, published on June 30, that began to cast doubt on Myra's innocence. I wrote that Brady had told

[2] Ian Craig, 'Good Lord', *Manchester Evening News*, July 22, 1985.
[3] 'Hindley denies other killings,' *The Observer*, August 4, 1985.

me that "The killing took place in the home of another man. It involves me. I'm not opting out. But the police can't prove it now because the house is demolished."

That morning Myra met Rena Duffy in the dispensary. She worked there as the orderly and Rena, who was trying to shed several stones, reported for her weekly weigh-in on the scales. They discussed the news on the radio, and Myra said of Brady: "I hate him. A few years ago he was talking about killing himself. I hoped he would kill himself, instead of just talking about it – get it over and done with. He can implicate me by just saying all this. After all, who is going to believe me?" She had a point: the world wanted to believe the worst of Myra Hindley. At this stage, however, she had not seen the *Sunday People*. The prisoners' copy had not been made available, that morning.

After tea that evening, the two friends met again in Myra's cell for a chat. Myra liked to confide in Rena, whom she had orginally met in Holloway 10 years previously. The East End girl, struggling to raise three children by herself, had succumbed to shoplifting. That is how she had come to be working in the kitchen in Holloway for a few months. Thanks to representations by Myra, Rena was transferred to a typing course.

By 8 p.m. Myra had read the confession in the newspaper. She told Rena that she knew Pauline and her mother, Joan Reade, but she denied knowing anything about the girl's disappearance. "I wouldn't leave that poor woman not knowing whether she was dead or alive, for 20 years. I was doing life already, so I had nothing to lose. If I knew anything, I would have told them," insisted Myra.

Then she made a bad mistake.

My story made no reference to Brady's allegation that David Smith was involved in Pauline's death. Nor did I mention 13 Wiles Street. The story confined itself to reporting Brady's claim that the girl had died in another man's house. That one fact, however, spoke volumes to Myra Hindley. She explained to Rena Duffy that the house to which Brady was referring was David Smith's home.

If Myra Hindley knew nothing about Pauline's death, how did she know that, cooped up in Cell 4 of the hospital wing of Gartree Prison, Ian Brady had identified 13 Wiles Street as the scene of the murder?

It could have been clever guesswork, of course, but that was an explanation that did not satisfy me. The murder trail, now more than 20 years old, was cold; even so, lady luck can sometimes spring a surprise. This time she came in the guise of Sister Doreen Wright.

*　*　*

Nursing was not a vocation for Doreen Wright. When she left her school in Highbury, North London, she went into accountancy. That proved to be a boring way to earn a living, so she decided to follow in her grandmother's steps and train as a nurse – "to see a bit of life". Her grandmother, Mrs Ester Lewis, who had been a nurse in China with the China Inland Mission, was sceptical about Doreen's willingness to apply herself. She was wrong, and her grand-daughter persevered with her training at Richmond Hospital until she qualified as a State Registered Nurse in 1954. The silver belt buckle which she wore to symbolise her graduation was the one worn by her grandmother in China. After her midwifery training at the West Middlesex Hospital, she found her way through hospitals and district nursing to Holloway, the prison for women in North London. She arrived there in 1966.

Sister Wright helped with an innovation in women's prisons: a crèche for babies. The crèche received excited attention in the media. The Press was fascinated that babies were in close proximity to notorious criminals. Holloway certainly had some infamous characters. E Block housed two of them: Ethel Gee and Helen Kruger, who were convicted of spying for Russia in 1961. They were joined by Myra Hindley, after her conviction for the Moors Murders, in May 1966. It was a few months after Myra's arrival in Holloway that Sister Wright, who was in charge of the psychiatric unit, received a phone call. Ethel Gee was suffering from indigestion pains.

Sister Wright prepared some medicine (Mag. Trisilicate) and crossed the courtyard into E Block. This account of what then happened is based on a Statutory Declaration sworn by Sister Wright before a Commissioner of Oaths.

A woman stopped me, and asked me if I wanted to look at her drawings, which had been hung on the walls in the common room. She said: "Would you like to look at my drawings?" They were quite good pencil sketches. I said "I'm sorry, I haven't got time". I had got time, in fact, but I felt a sudden feeling of not wanting to bother.

Instead, I went through a door and into the glass cubicle used by the prison officers who keep a watch on the inmates in this block. The cubicle had partition walls that were about eight feet high. I put down the medicine, and started talking to a prison officer. I asked the officer who the person was who had spoken to me, and she said "Myra Hindley". At first, I had thought she was a member of the staff dressed in civvies – she was so smart. Her hair was dark, and Myra's was blond in the photographs that were published at the time.

Suddenly, I heard shouting and I looked up. I saw Myra Hindley doing her nut. She had lost her rag. She was so angry, she didn't know what she was saying. She was looking at me, and calling me a snotty bugger, or something like that. Then she started ranting about someone called David Smith. I was familiar with the name, because of the Moors murder trial, but it didn't mean anything to me.

Myra said "I'll get that fucking David Smith. He helped us kill a 16-year-old girl that he was going with, and she's still on the moors. Her mother thinks that she might have gone off to Australia; she doesn't know she's dead. She's on the moors with the others. David Smith used to go out with her, and he got tired of her. We did her in Smith's house. We helped him get rid of her in his house, and they'll never find her. But when I get out I'm going to tell the police where she is."

I thought to myself "Blimey, it sounds like she thinks she's going out tomorrow". The other officer said "We are going to have trouble with her tonight". I also distinctly remember certain other phrases that Myra used. One was "There are other bodies up there". Another was her description of the police as "pigs and fucking idiots".

Somebody – I think it was Ethel Gee, with whom she was speaking – said something like "What age was she?" Myra said "Bloody 16 and he knows it". By this, I presumed that she meant that Smith knew more about the death than other people were aware of. Myra said "He had a girlfriend and he was tired of her. He wanted to get rid of her".

She said very distinctly that it happened in Smith's house. She repeated: "And I know where she is, and when I get out I'm going to get Smith for it". She also said: "He killed a fucking 16-year-old girl in his house, and he's got away with it. There's worse people outside than in". Also: "We did her in Smith's house because Smith had been going out with her". She started to laugh, and I thought at the time that she was a bit nuts.

She was angry because I had ignored her, so she blew her top. I did not know, at the time, that there was a 16-year-old girl who had gone missing. I did not know the name Pauline Reade, and she did not mention Pauline Reade's name.

I asked a prison officer if what Myra was saying was true, and she said "She's been ranting about that every time she loses her temper". I asked her if she had told anybody, and she said she had not, because the Official Secrets Act was strictly enforced in Holloway. And anyway, the governor was friendly towards Myra Hindley. Myra was saying it, and nobody in Holloway would believe her!

I was asked to wait for five minutes, while another officer went across to Myra to quieten her down. I then left, with two officers accompanying me through the common room. Myra Hindley tried to be friendly, as I passed, but I ignored her.

Although I was told by some officers that there were no other bodies on the moors, I was still worried about it. It was getting to me that there was a mother looking for a daughter, who thought that she had gone abroad. I did not go to the governor; she would not have believed me. It was this governor who took Myra out of Holloway for a ride in a taxi and a walk around a park.

The memory of that scene was still fresh in Sister Wright's mind when she attended the murder trial of Kim Newell at Oxford Assizes in June 1967. Newell, who was on remand in Holloway, was pregnant; that called for constant nursing attention, which was provided by Sister Wright.

During those proceedings I saw Mr Forbes, who I think was a detective inspector; he was involved in the Moors Murder investigation. On one occasion, I found myself sitting next to him, beneath the witness box. I asked him if there were any more bodies on the moors, and he said he did not think so – but he added that it was not his case. I thought he might have done something about what Myra Hindley had said, but his reaction was negative so I left it. Eventually, I convinced myself that "There aren't any more", but that incident with Myra Hindley stuck in my mind.

* * *

In its important detail, Sister Wright's statement is a carbon copy of Ian Brady's confession. Nonetheless, Myra Hindley might wish to argue that the story is a fabrication. If it transpires that Myra is correct, then Sister Wright is guilty of perjury, which is punishable in a court of law.

To seek corroboration, I went in search of Ethel Gee. On her release from prison, Gee married Harry Houghton, another member of the Portland spy ring. They sold their house in

Dorset, and re-settled further down the coast in Poole. When I arrived in Bushell Road, No 48 was empty. Ethel had died on June 7, 1984, and Harry died a few weeks before I knocked on his door. There was now no alternative except to fall back on an internal examination of Sister Wright's story, to establish the integrity of the evidence.

Sister Wright could have visited Manchester and, by diligent detective work, traced the Gorton girls who were scattered on the city's overspill estates. From them, she could have established that David Smith lived two doors away from Pauline, and that they were good friends. Furthermore, she could have learnt that, at the time of Pauline's disappearance, a rumour circulated in the Taylor Street area which suggested that the girl had gone to live in Australia.

But if her objective was to implicate Myra in another murder, why should she complicate her story by trying to smear David Smith? What would be her motive? He, so far as she knew, had performed a public service by tipping off the police. And having constructed this fantastic story in her mind, why did she harbour it in silence until I arrived at her home nearly 20 years later?

There is another crippling weakness in the hypothesis that Sister Wright fabricated her story: why should she settle for an unidentified 16-year-old girl, when she could have selected Keith Bennett as the victim? Keith's disappearance, which was well-publicised in Manchester, had all the classic hallmarks of the Moors murders imprinted on it.

But the one fact that is fatal to Myra Hindley's defence is Sister Wright's statement that the murder took place in Smith's house. To concoct that, Sister Wright would surely have had to possess remarkable powers of imagination. Perhaps she is fortunate to possess those powers. But in that case, what are the odds against her fabricating the same fact which, independently, was germinating in the tortured mind of Ian Brady?

Fortunately, however, we do not have to rely on speculation to arrive at a conclusion as to whether Sister Wright has given an accurate account of what Myra Hindley said on that day in

E Block, for we have uncovered a witness who has obliquely corroborated her story: Myra Hindley herself! Nineteen years after the intemperate meeting with Sister Wright in E Block, Myra Hindley repeated the statement that Pauline Reade died in Smith's house. This time she disclosed that nugget of information to Rena Duffy. In doing so she branded herself guilty of complicity in another murder.

*   *   *

I was now satisfied that Ian Brady's confession of a murder conspiracy had served to trap Myra Hindley, but I was far from convinced that I had been told the truth about David Smith. The Moors murderers, after all, had a perfect motive for smearing him: he was the man who put them behind bars. But if they were insisting that he was guilty, how could I prove a negative – that he was innocent?

CHAPTER EIGHT

Hand of Fate

Coming from Ian Brady and Myra Hindley, the accusation against David Smith had to be treated with extreme caution. They hate Smith with a ferocious intensity. To allow them to bear witness against him is like giving credence to the testimony of the mad Marquis de Sade himself! But before she died, Pauline Reade left a clue behind which troubled me. It was a clue which the police failed to uncover at the time of their investigation, and it pointed an accusing finger at 13 Wiles Street – David Smith's home.

Pauline's petite mother, Joan, carried the secret of that clue around with her for 22 years. Ever since 1963, barely a day goes by without her thinking back to the events of that evening in July when she waved goodbye to Pauline. It started with the police questions after she first raised the alarm; the questions continued after the conviction of Brady and Hindley, as reporters trooped through 9 Wiles Street in search of fresh details for their accounts of the Moors murders. And then, time and again, Mrs Reade has turned over the detail of her daughter's departure for the dance at the railwaymen's club as she reproved herself for not finding a companion for her. But the one vital, stark clue to what happened to her remained buried in the deep recesses of her anguished mind.

As I took her through a step by step account of events from the moment her husband Amos returned from the pub that evening, Mrs Reade let slip the story of how she found Pauline's white glove. I had not read about the glove in any of the reports of her disappearance, so I asked her to repeat the detail of that incident.

Earlier that summer Pauline went shopping with her mother to Gorton market for a pair of white linen gloves that matched her new dress. She wore them once to a dance at the railwaymen's club. On the night that Pauline disappeared, Mrs Reade found one of the gloves, which she tucked away in the sideboard in the kitchen. No, she had not informed the police, because she had forgotten all about it.

Mrs Reade says that she found the glove soon after 9 p.m. It was a warm evening, and she had opened the door to look casually up the street to see who was about. She spotted the glove, and thought to herself "Pauline must have dropped it when she went out." She stepped into the street and retrieved it. A few days later, she looked for the other glove. It was nowhere in the house. "I didn't tell the police. I was so upset thinking about Pauline."

I asked Mrs Reade to identify the precise location of the glove. It was about 9 feet away from her front door, in the gutter of the cobbled street. Facing outwards, the glove was at a 45 degrees angle to Mrs Reade's left.

From this account, I concluded that her assumption about when the glove was dropped in the gutter was incorrect. Two reasons lead to this view. The first is that Mrs Reade walked out of the front door of her house after Pauline, and returned through the same door within half-an-hour. On neither occasion did she see the snow-white glove. During her return journey to her house, she would have been walking straight towards the glove, which would have been staring her in the face. It is difficult to believe that she would have overlooked it. This implies that the glove was dropped during the hour after Mrs Reade's return to her house at 8.15 p.m.

The second reason for this deduction is that, in heading for the dance, Pauline would have turned right out of her front door. This would have taken her east along Wiles Street in the direction of Taylor Street. So if she dropped her glove at this stage, it ought to have been on the pavement to the right of the door.

If I am correct, we are now in a position to speculate about what happened to Pauline when she disappeared in Froxmer Street.

The easy explanation would be that she was lured into her friend Myra Hindley's car – also occupied by her boyfriend, Ian Brady – and driven round to Wiles Street. The car could have been parked outside No 11, between her house and David Smith's; and then, as she stepped out of the car, Pauline dropped her glove before entering No 13, there to be murdered by Ian Brady, Myra Hindley and (if they are to be believed) David Smith.

This reconstruction favours the Brady-Hindley allegation, but it does not have the ring of plausibility. Why should Brady, who was about to execute his first homicidal act with his lover Myra, run the risk of taking his victim to another man's house and even park the car within spitting distance of the girl's front door? If, as I eventually discovered, Brady had lied to me about Smith's involvement, could I offer a better explanation for the glove's presence in the gutter? I suspect that something like this happened.

Pauline Reade was worried about going to the dance by herself. She and her mother had made strenuous efforts to find one of the Gorton girls willing to accompany her. As Pauline walked down Froxmer Street, in the shadow of Beyer Peacock's wall, did she suddenly wonder if her friend Maureen Hindley would go with her? By this time, Maureen had established a close relationship with David Smith and she spent long hours with him in No 13.

Pauline could have turned round (which explains why she did not emerge in Railway Street), and within five minutes would have walked back along Gorton Lane, turned left into Charmers Street and sharp right into Wiles Street. This course would have taken her along the north side of Wiles Street until she was almost diametrically opposite her home, No 9. Then, she would have cut across the road at an angle, opposite No 11 – where the glove was found – and reached the pavement on the south side of the road near the door of No 9. Here, she could reasonably have expected to find Maureen with David. If she did not find Maureen at No 13, where would she go looking for her? Her sister Myra kept close tabs on Maureen, so might she have gone round to Granny Maybury's house in Bannock Street? There, she would have been introduced to Myra's live-in boyfriend, Ian Brady. Had Pauline already been identified by Myra as a threat to her baby sister Maureen's romance with David Smith? If so, there was a no-risk opportunity for Brady to strike in the privacy of his home.

Just over an hour later, Pauline's brother saw David Smith arguing with Maureen on the corner of Benster and Charmers Street. Myra was watching the incident from a distance. There was no sight of Ian Brady. The simplest test of David Smith's innocence was the date on which he first met Ian Brady. If their first meeting took place *after* Pauline's disappearance, the teenager could hardly have been implicated in the murder of his friend Pauline.

David Smith vividly recalls the first occasion that he met Myra's laconic boyfriend. It happened at Millwards, where Maureen had gone to work with her sister. During an office party one of the men had got fresh with Maureen and made some fruity suggestions to her. Maureen took some delight in relating the detail to her pugnacious boyfriend. He, true to form, decided to make the man eat his words with the help of a knuckle sandwich. So David lay in wait outside Millwards one lunchtime, but he failed to catch sight of his quarry. He returned at 5 p.m. and spotted the man emerging from a side door. He gave chase, but the man (who had been alerted to his fate by Maureen) escaped across the car park. David glared after him, and heard Myra call to him. She offered him a lift home. He climbed into the car, and was introduced to Ian Brady.

When did this incident occur? David cannot remember the precise date, but he thought that it was a few months before his marriage to Maureen in the summer of 1964 – a long time after Pauline disappeared.

I tried to verify David Smith's claim that he had not met Brady during the summer of 1963, but none of the Gorton residents

whom I traced could be emphatic. They held the cautious view
expressed by Linda Bradshaw, a chatty blond girl who was one
of Myra's neighbours in Bannock Street. "I am pretty sure
Smith didn't know Brady at the time," she says.

It was an examination of the record of the trial at Chester
Assizes that conclusively branded Ian Brady a liar – and finally
satisfied me that David Smith was innocent of murder. Brady
was being questioned by his Counsel, Mr Emlyn Hooson QC,
on Friday, April 29, 1966, when he was asked for the date on
which he first met Smith. Brady was precise in his answer:
October 1963, when Smith called at the offices of Millwards.
Brady does not make mistakes. He is fastidious about detail.
This was illustrated a week later, when Judge Fenton Atkinson
asked him if he had anything to say before sentence was passed.
Brady had his final platform, and the world was waiting for his
every word. He could have vented his anger against authority,
denounced the jury, justified his actions, pleaded for mercy, or
one of a number of other responses of the sort that people
deliver before being condemned to prison for life. Not Ian
Brady. "Nothing," he said, "except the revolvers were bought
in July 1964." The court had been misled, and before departing
for a lifetime's incarceration Mr Brady pedantically insisted on
correcting a detail in the official record.

*   *   *

Brady and Hindley concocted their devious plot against the
prosecution's chief witness while waiting for trial. They had
ample opportunity to elaborate the detail of their smear as they
sat next to each other during the committal proceedings in the
magistrates court. It was at this stage that Brady says he
fabricated the story which was to serve as Myra's defence
against the charge of murder.

The most convincing lies have elments of verifiable truth in
them, however, and that was the case with the story that Ian
Brady whispered into my ears in Gartree 20 years later. At the
heart of that story was the claim that the most damaging

evidence against Smith was the blood in 13 Wiles Street.

The police tore 13 Wiles Street apart after they had charged Ian Brady with murder. The concrete floor in the kitchen was dug up, and the wallpaper was stripped off for forensic examination. The police did find traces of blood, and Brady was questioned about it. So was Smith, and he explained that the blood was his. What is more, he had perfect alibis: his friend Pauline's brother, Paul, and her mother, Mrs Joan Reade. This is the story that they told me:

About two months after Pauline disappeared, Smith was installing a new pane of glass in the window of his living room. By now, he was the sole occupant of the house. His old landlady, Miss Jones, had long since departed to another world, and his itinerant father was away on his travels.

David's hand slipped, and he cut his wrist on the glass. He began to bleed profusely. He went to the door and looked out. Paul Reade was coming down the road.

"Is your mum in?" asked Smith.

"Yes. Why, what's the matter?" replied Paul.

"I've cut my wrist."

Paul, who did not like the sight of blood, glanced at the hand. "I'll get my old lady," he said, and quickly stepped into No 9.

Mrs Reade rushed to No 13, and found the careless young David flicking his hand. "The blood was going all over the place," recalls Mrs Reade. She put the boy's hand under the tap, and then took him round to her house to bandage the cut.

The bloodstains remained on the walls; stains which excited the police two years later. But when they challenged him, he took them next door for a talk with Mrs Reade.

The other strands in Brady's fabricated story are not so easy to understand. He said that David and Maureen had a dress belonging to Pauline. Maureen and Pauline knew each other as children, but Mrs Reade could not recall her daughter ever lending a dress to the Hindley girl. At no stage has anyone ever suggested that Maureen knew what her sister and Brady were up to as they cruised the streets of Manchester in their cars and vans. Is it conceivable that David would produce a dress that belonged to Pauline, without making Maureen suspicious? On the other hand, did Brady keep Pauline's party dress as evidence that he had completed his murder mission?

Myra Hindley, in her version, claimed that Pauline was murdered because Smith wanted to get rid of a troublesome girlfriend. But at the time of her disappearance the shy Pauline was not competing with Maureen Hindley for the affections of David Smith. Maureen's relationship with David was well established, and Pauline posed no threat. At least, she was not perceived as a threat by her friends, by her mother or by David Smith. But what if Brady asked Myra to nominate a victim, someone whose disappearance she would be able to easily verify (the disappearance constituting proof that Brady had carried out his part of the deed)? Who better than Pauline, the girl whom Myra – protective of her younger sister's interests – fancifully thought might come between Maureen and her boyfriend?

* * *

Even if Mrs Reade had informed the police about the glove that Pauline had dropped outside No 11 Wiles Street, this clue would have been insufficient to lead them to the couple who were to become infamous as the Moors murderers.

If the glove pointed at No 13 Wiles Street, then the police discharged their duty by thoroughly examining David Smith's house. They did initially consider the possibility that he was associated with the disappearance of Pauline Reade, but they found no evidence whatsoever to sustain such a suspicion.

We are, however, left with one final puzzle over the murder of Pauline Reade. Brady was anxious to stress, for my benefit, that she did not die in Granny Maybury's house in Bannock Street. He insisted that the girl died in Smith's house which – because it had been demolished – could not now bear witness against them. But did the police examine 7 Bannock Street? According to the account by Emlyn Williams:

"Report from Nimmo, Manchester City: 13 Wiles Street,

now empty, had been searched from rotten floorboard to peeling ceiling, and even Tyrrell hadn't found a sausage. 'And why' said Talbot, 'did the Corporation have to pull down 7 Bannock Street just to spite the police?'[1]

Was Brady's house really not examined by the detectives and their forensic experts? According to Manchester City Corporation records, the odd numbered houses in Bannock Street were not demolished until August 1972 – seven years after Brady's arrest. They were still standing when the police were tearing David Smith's house apart.

Drawing on his fading memory, Arthur Benfield, who at the time was the Chief Superintendent in charge of Cheshire's detectives, thought that Bannock Street had been demolished by the time they slammed Brady behind bars. I asked Robert Talbot, the superintendent who had the distinction of arresting Brady, if he had been quoted accurately by playwright Emlyn Williams. Mr Talbot, now living in retirement in the lovely medieval town of Chester, refused to comment. He was weary – and wary – of being pestered about the case. "Discretion tells me to leave it alone."

If the police had conducted a forensic examination of 7 Bannock Street, would they have found traces of the blood of Pauline Reade?

* * *

When, in the annals of criminal history, has one man had the privilege of serving as the instrument for denouncing the same murderers on two occasions separated by 20 years? Such has been David Smith's unique role. The first time was when he telephoned the police in 1965 after witnessing the bloody destruction of Edward Evans. Smith had no control over the timing of the second occasion. Ian Brady and Myra Hindley, in their determination to relish revenge, weaved a murder plot to implicate their accuser; Ian Brady, in triggering that plot in 1985, succeeded only in exposing himself and his former lover for what would otherwise have been a perfect murder.

[1] Williams, *op. cit.*, p. 332.

PART THREE

The Cult

CHAPTER NINE

Homicide as Ritual

Ian Brady knew that he was special. He did not *feel* the same way as ordinary people; that was at the heart of the matter. His rejection of society's moral values and conventions was the defiant act of an outcast. But something was missing; he lacked zest. Everything was grey and lifeless. Then he met Myra Hindley, which was what he now describes as a "rejuvenation": a new lease of life.

Their courtship was no ordinary affair, for although they shared the same bed, sex and romance was not a strong enough bond to tie them together. He needed something extra to stimulate his sexual emotions to a level that would arouse Myra and cement their relationship forever.

Sadism provided that stimulant. Ian Brady's emotionally deprived childhood produced the classic inferiority complex that manifested itself in shallow social contact with others. This in turn led to hostility towards people in general, a hostility which he channelled into his private perversions. He systematically excluded others from his life and scorned the values that are generally accepted by society.

It is not true that everyone who suffers from emotional deprivation early in life subsequently turns to sadism for relief. Some do, and these people constitute a group which has been analysed by Alfred Adler, an Austrian psychologist who broke away from Sigmund Freud to establish what he called the school of Individual Psychology. In his view, there is one type of person who can be tempted into sadism – those in whom tension caused by fright produces sexual excitement. Hertha Orgler summarised Adler's thesis in these terms:

Sadists produce their tension by identifying themselves with their victim. The fact that only discouraged individuals, who do not trust themselves to solve the love problem in normal fashion, choose this path is often disputed by pointing out that sadists are brutal. Adler refutes this by indicating that they always choose children or other defenceless individuals as their victims; that is to say, that their sexual desire takes the way of least resistance.[1]

Ian Brady's pathological behaviour, however, was not restricted to a simple case of sadism. Underpinning it was a spiritualism. This transformed a psychopath, whose self-control periodically collapsed into random killings, into a programmed murderer. But Brady's spiritualism needed a catalyst before it could fuse with his psychoses to unleash evil. That catalyst was Myra Hindley.

Myra gave meaning to Ian's meaningless life. Now he could share all his secrets. She was introduced to The Face of Death, and tutored in the deeds that lead to Napoleonic immortality. Ian Brady had his bride for eternity, a union that he perversely consecrated with the death of Pauline Reade.

★ ★ ★

Ian and Myra created a crazy cult – a killing cult. The sadistic slaughter of children was ritualised to provide the stimulus to their personal relationship and also to appease The Face of Death, to which they were spiritual slaves.

The sacrifices were offered on an average once every six months. The timetable was the product of two pressures. One was the need periodically to renew the personal relationship between Myra and Ian. The other was to relieve the psychotic stress within Brady.

Ian schooled Myra into the routine preparations for their

[1]Hertha Orgler, *Alfred Adler: The Man and his Work*, London: Sidgwick and Jackson, 1973, p. 145.

nights of orgy. First, all incriminating evidence had to be removed from their home. It was packed in suitcases and secreted at the left luggage office of one of the railway stations.

Then, Brady compiled lists of instructions: the assembly of materials that they needed (such as protective clothing), the purchase of Pro-Plus, a mild stimulant available at drug stores, and the preparation of an alibi in case anything went wrong. Finally, they planned the detail for disposing of the bodies down to the need to count the number of buttons on the victim's clothes. Ian Brady was meticulous in his attention to detail. A stray button accidentally left behind in their house could – at that time – lead to the gallows.

Brady had already found the cemetery – his God's Garden: Saddleworth Moor, a steady one-hour drive from Bannock Street. Here, Myra's "flowers" could be planted in the water-logged peat at the heart of their spiritual universe, their souls sucked screaming into hell by Brady's Face of Death. The tranquillity that descended on Brady as he stalked the moors, however, his eyes staring darkly through tinted glasses, was occasionally shattered by the intrusion of God – the God of the world religions. Brady professed to be an atheist, but without warning he could be tormented by a power that was mightier than his Face of Death. He recalled one such incident for me.

He was standing on the brow of a hill, the wind sweeping back his long brown hair. Beneath him were the graves of children. He raised his fist and blasphemed the heavens.

"I was laughing and crying at the same time," he said. "I was supposed to be an atheist, but I was in fact saying 'Hey, you bastard', which was acknowledging that there was something higher.

"There was nothing in the sky. I was saying, in effect, 'Take that, you fucker'."

Ian Brady's defiant gesture with his fist was a betrayal of the cult that he created with Myra. It was, he admitted, a "grotesque" thing for him to do; grotesque because, fleetingly, it acknowledged a personal God, an acknowledgement which undermined the crazy logic of his creed.

Myra passed her driving test on November 7, 1963. Their second sacrifice was delivered two weeks later, on Friday November 23, 1963, seven months after the death of Pauline Reade.

Emlyn Williams, in his account of the murders, suggests that the assassination in Dallas of President John F. Kennedy the previous day had a psychological impact on Brady which impelled him to go out and kill.[2] If this was true, it weakens the thesis that the killing cult had established a dynamic of its own. We would be back to the explanation that the murders were random events in which there was no logic underpinning the periodicity of deaths. I asked Brady if the Williams theory was correct. "It had nothing to do with Kennedy," he replied. "That was not the trigger."

The murder, of course, might have been an unconscious reaction to the news that left the world dumbstruck. Ian, however, had already taken the decision to kill. On Thursday, after work, Myra drove him to one of the central stations to deposit a suitcase. As he walked through the concourse he heard the first mention of the assassination.

"I passed two passengers, and I heard one say to the other 'Did you hear about Kennedy?', and then the word 'dead'.

"The girl was in the car park and as soon as I got in, I switched on the radio and found out he was dead."

Was he affected emotionally by Kennedy's death, like everyone else? "No," said Brady emphatically. "When I heard that Tommy Cooper had died, or Eric Morecombe had died, it meant something, you know, because they gave happiness and you are affected by them.

"You hear some dictator or some foreign politician in America has died or been assassinated, and it means nothing to you. But people who give pleasure or you've respect for, and you hear that they're dead, you have the same feeling as anybody else."

John Kilbride, a blue-eyed boy with dark brown hair, was the eldest of seven children. He lived with his parents in

[2] Williams, *op. cit,*. pp. 170, 348.

Smallshaw Lane, Ashton-under-Lyne. He left home with 3s and a penknife in his pocket to visit the Pavilion to see a film called *The Moguls*. John was not a bright lad; he was receiving remedial lessons at school. But he had a cheerful smile. He detoured to the local market to earn 3d by helping stall-holders. He was wearing a sports jacket, white shirt and neatly pressed grey flannel trousers. He was not seen again.

How Ian and Myra killed him we do not know. His body was too badly decomposed when it was finally exhumed from its acid grave on the moors. All we can be sure of is that Ian lured John into a car that was hired and driven by Myra.

★   ★   ★

Myra's car served as the hearse for their murder rituals. It was deployed to pick up the victims, return them to Granny Maybury's home, and then transport the bodies to God's Garden. Their travels in the car had a mystical quality for them. The car concealed the lovers from the world. Ian spoke about it at length to one psychiatrist, who recorded in his report:

> The car was like a shelter to them. It carried them about safely. He instanced one occasion when they sat in the car and watched the crowds go by – he knowing what they had done and exhilarated by the secret – they were cut off in the car and the outside crowd were in ignorance of the occupants. This was a powerful and liberating feeling.

Safely behind the closed doors of their satellite they orbited their fantasy world in peace, free from the constraints that shackled lesser mortals. Brady symbolised this freedom when he ordered Myra to park outside Strangeways Prison, in the centre of Manchester, to heighten their sense of spiritual liberation.

"We watched prisoners in their windows swinging lines from cell to cell," he told me. "This was their way of passing tobacco and newspapers to one another. They were too far away to make out the faces, of course, but you could hear the voices.

"We were just sat there, a nice sunny evening, in the car, smoking cigarettes, drinking wine. That wine tasted beautiful because we were watching people in prison."

In February 1964 Myra bought another car, and they travelled to Scotland for their Easter holiday. The visits to the countryside, particularly the Lake District which was within an easy drive for a weekend outing, were regular occurrences. Their favourite destinations were in Scotland, where Ian could retrace his childhood trips. He took Myra to the ruins of the castle at St. Monance, the sandy-beached resort in the mouth of the Firth of Forth looking out into the North Sea, and showed her the old stone bridge at Dunning, in the Ochil Hills above Perth.

But it was the wild terrain, the granite outcrops of the mountain chains of the north, that enraptured Ian. Here, he left his physical marks on nature – usually bullets (.45, .38 and .22s) lodged in trees, fired at rocks and even into a railway sleeper that had been abandoned by workmen who laid the North Sea gas pipeline. These material objects – a wine bottle sunk into a moorland stream, a Gordon's Gin bottle pushed into a hedge – were markers of his presence in the nature that he revered.

The return journeys took them through Glasgow, where Ian re-lived his street corner escapades; the texture of the brownstone tenements seemingly came alive to his touch. And then back to Millwards and the invoices, studiously conforming to the office routine without so much as a hint that they had been on a secret sojourn into the darkness of the night.

* * *

By the middle of June 1964, six months after the death of John Kilbride, Ian and Myra were ready for their next sacrifice. On the 18th, 12-year-old Keith Bennett said goodbye to his mother Winnie on Stockport Road. They had walked from their home in Eston Street, Longsight. His mother was going to bingo, and

Keith was walking to his gran's home, half-a-mile away, where he was going to spend the night.

Ian had visited his mother in Westmoreland Road, near the treacle factory, and was being driven down Stockport Road. He told Myra to pull over, and beckoned the fair-haired boy to the van. Keith, a short-sighted lad who wore spectacles, was wearing a white leather jacket over his T-shirt, and blue jeans. He climbed into the vehicle, and was never seen again. Ian refused to admit to detectives that he and Myra knew anything about the boy's disappearance. All that he would say to me was this: "I was involved. She was involved."

That autumn was bad for Ian. He was rapidly becoming bored with life. There was some relief in September, because Granny Maybury was allocated a house on the new overspill estate in Hattersley. They occupied themselves with the packing, and then there was the excitement of moving in to the end-of-terrace house, 16 Wardle Brook Avenue.

Their new neighbours, the Braithwaites, were from Jamaica; this did not please Ian or Myra, who strongly resented this close proximity of black people. Nonetheless, the house offered some interesting diversions. There was a small tree-filled valley just a short walk across the estate, over the brow of the hill. Ian enjoyed his saunters in the valley with the two dogs, Lassie and Puppet. In addition, the small garden offered the prospect of growing flowers and perhaps some vegetables. The clay soil was not fertile, but that was easily remedied: they made regular expeditions to the moors to collect bags of peat to mix into the clay.

A melancholic depression descended on Ian as the Yuletide festivities approached. It usually happened, this time of the year, when families were excitedly preparing for the gift-giving season. Children seemed happier, and the shops lit up with the dazzling lights and decorations. All of this served to twist the knot tighter in Ian's mind.

He sought diversion by taking pornographic photographs of Myra and himself. They locked themselves in a bedroom, so that Granny Maybury could not accidentally walk in and discover their secret. Myra used to don a hood with two eye slits, but this was eventually discarded so that Ian's lens could capture her naked, lying on the bed, the red weals left by a whip fully exposed on her back. Ian photographed himself urinating against a curtain.

To all outward appearances, the occupants of 16 Wardle Brook Avenue made the usual preparations for Christmas Day. But this was not a conventional religious occasion for Ian Brady and Myra Hindley; they were atheists, and they would not go to church to acknowledge the birth of Jesus. A few minutes before midnight, on Christmas Eve, Myra walked 20 yards down the path from her front door to the home of 12-year-old Pat Hodges, who regularly accompanied them to the moors. Earlier that evening, Pat had been in No 16, drinking the whisky, gin and wine offered by Ian. When the pair decided to spend midnight on the moors, seeing in Christmas Day by communing with nature, they agreed to take Pat with them. The girl's mother had no objection, and the three of them sat quietly in the van, drinking wine from a bottle, as the minutes ticked away into Christmas Day.

Ian was happy. He wanted to spend the night on the moors, but first they had to return Pat to her home. They collected blankets from No 16 and were back on the bleak hilltop of God's Garden to keep company with Myra's little flowers beneath the peat.

Saturday, December 26: Boxing Day. A public holiday, in which people became spectators at football matches, or recovered from the gastronomic excesses of Christmas by snoozing in front of the television. Leslie Ann Downey wanted to go to the fair in Hulme Hall Lane with her friend Linda Clarke. She wrapped a cardigan and blue coat over her tartan dress, and with 6d in her pocket she went out into the snow as dusk was settling over her home in Charnley Walk, Ancoats.

The fair was a 10-minute walk away. She spent her coins on the amusements, and was then split from her group of friends. Ian and Myra spotted her in the crowd, by herself, and it was while she was on her way home that they lured her into their van. They offered to take her for a drive, which ended up in Wardle Brook Avenue.

There, in a bedroom, Ian erected his studio lights and started the tape recorder which was concealed beneath the bed. Myra brought Lesley Ann into the room, and Ian forced her to undress. She became terrified and begged to be sent home. As the harrowing minutes ticked by, the tape recorded the defilement of Lesley Ann Downey, a slim little blue-eyed girl who was being used to gratify Ian's lust. There were gurgling sounds and heavy breathing as one of them held the child by the neck.

Lesley Ann pleaded to Myra, addressing her as if she were her mother. "Please mum, please – I cannot tell you. I cannot breathe . . . Please God . . . Why? What are you going to do with me?"

Ian then told her that he wanted to take some photographs. "I have got to get home before 8 o'clock. I have got to get . . . or I will get killed if I don't, honest to God."

God could not help Lesley Ann in the house of horror. She had been selected as a sacrifice to The Face of Death. After Ian finished taking his photographs, with Lesley Ann dressed in nothing more than socks and shoes and a gag that Myra had stuffed into her mouth, he placed Myra's pillow over her face and smothered her to death.

* * *

During their first two years together as lovers, Ian and Myra killed four young people: two a year, one in the summer, the other in the winter. The deaths were ritualised sacrifices that were designed to "gain credit" with The Face of Death. This is the first characteristic of a cult: it is auto-soteric – that is, it provides a system of self-salvation. Ian Brady, and his convert Myra Hindley, explicitly sought salvation in the after-life by sending ahead of them the souls of young people.

It made sense for Brady to locate The Face of Death on the moors. Pantheism subverts the foundations of religion and morality and entails the deification of sin. This spiritual philosophy merged perfectly into Brady's destructive personality.

That his cyclical homicides were ritualised can be perceived from a characteristic which has been defined in one psychiatric textbook in these terms:

> Where there are rituals there is usually also *Folie de Doute*, i.e. the doubt that the ritual has not been carried through according to prescription.[3]

Ian and Myra devised several mechanisms for allaying their doubts. One was to prepare lists of instructions, the *Aide Memoire*, against which their actions could be checked. In the list that constituted his plan to kill and dispose of Edward Evans, for example, Brady wrote: "Check periodically on move".

In addition, they took photographs of the graves. These provided a permanent record which could be consulted for reassurance. One of these photographs proved to be crucial in convicting Myra: she posed with her dog directly above John Kilbride's grave. One of the prized possessions of the cult was a tartan album full of photographs of God's Garden: sweeping vistas with no intrinsic merit to anyone except the initiated.

The regular trips to the moors to sit and drink wine near the graves were also part of the process of reminding themselves that they had faithfully performed the rites of their mad cult.

But it did not stop at that. Brady liked to mix reassurance with a cruel morbidity. This took the form of a macabre intrusion on the grief of the victim's family. John Kilbride's mother, Sheila, was subjected to this sick curiosity a month after her son disappeared. Ian and Myra called at her home in Smallshaw Lane posing as detectives. For half-an-hour they gratified their curiosity by asking Mrs Kilbride questions about John, such as which school he attended. The killers did not fear

[3] Slater and Roth, *op cit.*, p. 132.

fate by walking into their victim's home to glean what
stimulation they could from the family's distress. As they left,
Ian said: "I will see you next week. Johnny will be with you".
They took away some of the boy's clothing, and were never seen
again.

★   ★   ★

But the thrill of the murders was now beginning to lose its
cutting edge for Ian Brady. He wanted to expand his circle of
worshippers, which meant sharing his secrets: a dangerous step
to take, indeed, but he believed that he had found a likely
convert to his cult in Myra's brother-in-law, David Smith.

CHAPTER TEN

The Killing Creed

Annie Smith died in 1962. David learnt the news while he was on his way to Gary's, his Uncle Alf's transport hotel where his grandmother was convalescing from treatment for cancer. As he stepped off the bus, an old man who was sitting on a wall called out to him, "You know your mum's dead?".

It hurt. That was no way to learn that your mum has died, and without saying goodbye. But the day got worse. Inside, the whole family was gathered. David thought their anguish was hypocritical.

"Do you want to see your mum?" his Aunt Bettie asked him, and she took him into the bedroom. The colour in the old woman's cheeks was already gone. Never again would she smile for young David.

The boy, now aged 14, walked into a nearby park. He was bitter. "She had no right to die," he told himself. "She didn't struggle for me, and she left it to some old bloke to tell me."

The bitterness intensified when David was banned from the funeral. To this day he does not know why that decision was taken. All he knew, at the time, was that "I wanted to see my old lady go down. I had slept with her in the attic. And they stopped me". Now he was on his own.

He yearned for friends, boys and girls, but his reputation kept him apart from them. Yes, he could join the gang, but that was because he was good with his right fist. It always helped to have a hard man on your side when it came to measuring up against neighbourhood gangs, but David wanted more than that; he wanted to be able to relax with close friends. Something was stirring inside him. He liked boys, but in a way that he could not acknowledge in Gorton. There was no way in which he was going to allow himself to get a reputation of being "a poof" among the youths who wanted any excuse to prove their manliness by knocking him down.

The girls seemed to like David. They knew he was rough and tough, and yet there was something gentle about him that appealed to them. Outwardly, in his leather wear or donkey jacket with the turned-up collars, he appeared to be brash. But he had style. He did not plod; when he walked, it was with a nice bounce on the balls of his feet. When he was with girls in Sivori's he could curl up – his legs crossed, his hand with the long fingernails propping up his chin – and be attentive to his companion. And in the pubs he drank vodka and lime, which was definitely not a man's drink.

With his grandmother dead, David feared that the courts might force him to live in his uncle's hotel. He was alone, now, in Wiles Street, where he spent as much time as he could with his girlfriend, Maureen Hindley. He decided the safest way to preserve his independence was to make Maureen pregnant. "I tried for a long time to get her pregnant. I held her hands above her head, so that I could leave it in, so she didn't have any choice."

In the evenings he escaped from his stomping grounds in Gorton to the cafes and pubs in Longsight. Here, during his final year at school, David flirted with two boys. There was sexual contact, but not a full-blown homosexual experience. The emotional companionship was more important than the physical experiments. Each affair was short-lived, however, and it was back to the street fights and sex with Maureen in Wiles Street.

"She was a giddy person," recalls David. "I could talk to her. She was a fighter – rough. No-one in the area had beaten Maureen in a fight. She was not an easy lay."

Then, in October 1963, Maureen complained to him that one of the men at Millwards had made unwelcome advances to her. David had thrashed people for less reason than that. The following lunchtime, armed with a thick blade, he was waiting in Levenshulme Road for the man to leave his office. But

Maureen, pleased at the prospect of her honour being defended, made the mistake of warning her suitor of his impending good hiding. He ducked out of the office through a back door.

David was back at Millwards at 5 p.m. His quarry spotted him across the car park and ran: David went in hot pursuit, but lost him.

Ian and Myra had just got into the mini van when they saw David in fruitless pursuit across the car park. When the boy gave up, Ian said to Myra: "Call him over, and offer him a lift." Myra did as she was told, and David climbed into the back of the van with the vaguest hint of a nod at the Scotsman. The fateful meeting had taken place.

* * *

The lanky Scotsman on his small motorcycle was an amusing sight to David. Several times, while playing Beatles and Rolling Stones records in Johnny Booth's house opposite Granny Maybury's, he saw tin cans tied to the machine. Youths had taken it for joy-rides, and Ian hit on the idea of fitting the cans onto the rear wheel so that he could hear anyone tampering with it.

In November 1963 he directed Myra to join Cheadle Rifle Club, which seemed a sensible way to find out how pistols could be purchased without him having to obtain a gun licence.

Maureen, meanwhile, had at long last become pregnant. David, however, was having difficulty in holding down his job as a labourer. He was working for Jim Miller, who ran a property repair business from his home in Railway Street. Jim had been good to him. On one occasion, when David gave his father "a good hiding", Mr Miller allowed the boy to stay at his home overnight until tempers cooled. David and Maureen spent many happy evenings as baby-sitters for the Millers' two children.

Jim Miller finally sacked David for his bad time-keeping. A few weeks later, on a Sunday morning, Myra knocked on his door. "David is out in the car with Maureen and my boyfriend," she said to Mr Miller. "Maureen is pregnant and they are going to get married, will you give him his job back?"

David was also about to appear in court. "If you give him the job back, he'll probably get off," said Myra.

Jim Miller was a soft touch. "OK, as long as he comes at 8 o'clock in the mornings."

David reported for work, but his time-keeping did not improve; he was fired again. That evening, under the influence of alcohol, David returned to the house, banged on the door and began shouting. "You rotten bastard. Myra's boyfriend will fucking get you. He's a Scot. He'll kill you."

Maureen was in bed in the Miller's house. The young couple had been fighting and Maureen was frightened, so they encouraged her to stay the night. Because of David's behaviour outside on the pavement, Maureen was ordered to dress and leave.

David and Maureen were married at the local register office on August 15. Myra and Ian were not guests, but that evening Myra arrived in Wiles Street with a message. "Ian would like a drink with you."

The couple smartened themselves up and walked round to Bannock Street. Granny Maybury had dutifully absented herself. Ian took photographs of themselves in groups of three. David had difficulty in understanding Ian's heavy Scottish accent, and what he could understand he thought was dumb. But he was impressed by Ian's three-piece suit. "Everybody was dressed up, but no-one was going anywhere. It was civilized and that impressed me."

The youth was introduced to one of Ian's drinking eccentricities. He placed a bottle of red wine next to the gas fire. When the bottle over-heated, the cork popped out and he drank the wine.

Myra was in fine spirits. With her skirt well above her knees – the mini was "in" – she leaned forward from her armchair and offered lots of advice to her Mo.

Two days later, Ian and Myra took the newly-weds on a

honeymoon trip to the Lake District. They sailed on Bowness, and Ian snapped away with his camera. As they toured about, the two men sat with the wine bottles in the back seat, and the Hindley sisters chatted away between themselves in the front.

The long Odyssey to murder had begun. David did not know it, at the time. All he knew was that he had found his special friend. The year before, he grew to realise that he was "split"; sexually, he liked both girls and boys. No, he was not a homosexual; nor did he like the term bi-sexual, which he felt was also too strong for his proclivities. He did not know what label to attach to the stirrings inside him, but they left him deeply confused.

"I occasionally met people away from my area of Gorton. It felt nice and very different to be with these boys. It became my nature to be generous. I enjoyed it. To bump shoulders, a little teasing, felt comforting. I got a buzz out of it that only I knew about, not like a poof, just a little buzz that was nice and private. But then some situation would arise and the old violence would be the answer."

The confusions evaporated when he started the weekend rides in the back seat with Ian Brady.

"Oh, the friendship, all new and different. Riding in cars, going places, girls in the front, us boys in the back, laughing, drinking whisky and good old vino, guns in holsters, slapping knees and shoulders at something either whisky sick or vino funny; Jesus, and that split felt like it was gone forever. In its place the buzz of teasing a friend, arms around shoulders like buddies, only Myra didn't like it too much, relegated to girls' talk with baby sister, but I didn't care – even that was part of the buzz and the tease.

"At night, the girls upstairs, the boys together downstairs; curling up to sleep on the couch, him on the chair, never approaching me to touch, a wife upstairs, a friend close by, no frustrations, nobody getting hurt. I think I felt just contented enough to be impressed out of my mind."

Ian was generous with the wine which he brought round to Wiles Street. They drank late into the evening until it was time to order the girls to bed. They then played 3-card brag. Ian usually lost. Wine, wine, wine. When they tired of cards, Ian borrowed David's starting pistol: he was impressed by the loud report. They would go outside to urinate behind the lock-up garages, on the other side of the street, and Ian would shatter the midnight silence with the pistol.

"Come here," he said one night to David. He pulled the boy across the road until they were standing underneath the street's single gas lamp. Then he pointed to No 9. "What do you think happened to that girl?"

David, who was well plastered with German wine, had no intelligent answer. The ghoulish gas-lit scene was enacted several times more in the following months. Ian – not yet ready to share his secret with his new friend – bathed in the glow of the gaslight and savoured the memory of his heroic deed, as Joan and Amos Reade were kept awake in their bed by the anguish of not knowing what had happened to Pauline.

*   *   *

Conversations during the late-night drinking sessions rambled aimlessly around any subject that the wine encouraged. Ian discoursed on world affairs, and employed theoretical concepts that impressed David.

Ian knew the boy's criminal record, and he began to ask vague questions that posed the possibility of violence. "How would you like a lot of money?" was one of his opening gambits, which threaded its way through to "What would you be prepared to do for money?"

David was anxious to please and impress his friend. "On looking back, it's easy to see the obvious, but to do that is a big mistake. To me, the full picture was never that obvious. Nothing stuck out as plainly evil. Time wasn't easily measured in separate days, it just flowed into one mass event. Time didn't stand still long enough to notice the difference between all the rights and all the wrongs."

Ian Brady knew that, for David Smith to be a fully-fledged

member of his cult, he had to transform the boy's personality. A cold heart was of more use than a hot temper. There was no room for uncontrolled actions: every move had to be calculated from beginning to end, the full permutation of consequences balanced in the equation to maximise the chances of success.

The process of transforming David Smith's attitudes and personality was a slow and subtle one, but it was working. He introduced the youth to the sort of guns he only saw in the cinema. The Smith and Wesson felt heavy but good in his hand. Up on the moors, Ian gave him plenty of target practice, shooting at rocks. In the surrounding fields, they fired at trees and fence posts. Ian demonstrated how to produce a dum dum bullet: he cut a deep cross in the nose of the bullet, and fired at a sheep which stood staring at them, a vacant look in its eyes. Half of the carcass blew out of the animal's side. David said he wanted a Luger, so the four of them drove up to Barnsley to buy one. The supplier, alas, was out. Still, he had access to Ian's guns.

Dreams were made of this stuff: wine, women and song, and the camaraderie of the charismatic Scot who was generous with his money. "I got my friend, all right," says Smith, "all grown up and worldly – compared to me, anyway. The violence was still around, but at the time I probably didn't realise what shape it was taking. Instead of a knife, it became a gun, but so what? Nobody was getting hurt, just popping-off the odd sheep and blowing apart the occasional oildrum or railway sleeper. That wasn't violence at all, was it?"

An atmosphere evolved between the two of them that David relished. He teased his friend, bumping his shoulders as they walked down the road. Ian had a gangly walk and slight stoop of shoulders, while David walked tall, with springs under his feet. Ian did not know what to make of the body language. He got embarrassed quickly, and admonished his young friend with friendly reprimands. "Lay off!"

There was little in common between them. Ian thought that David's preference in music – the heavy guitars of Duane Eddy – was rubbish. He preferred Glen Miller. They dressed differently: Ian in his conservative grey attire, while David tried hard to replicate the sulky James Dean look. Their eating habits contrasted sharply, too. Ian enjoyed mushy food like macaroni cheese out of a Heinz tin, or tomatoes on toast; David liked red-blooded meat and potatoes. But their relationship seemed to gel, which accentuated the friction between Myra and David. "I didn't care," says David. "Even that was part of the buzz and the tease."

After Ian and Myra moved to Hattersley, they regularly returned to Wiles Street to maintain the stream of alcohol, laced with half-baked philosophy and tantalising plots about how to make easy money. The euphoria was shattered with the death, six months after she was born, of baby Angela Dawn. David was at work when he received a message to say that Maureen was in hospital in hysterics. He did not think that anything serious had happened, so he dawdled on his way to Ancoats Hospital. When he arrived he was told that the baby had died. He tore the hospital room to shreds; even the lamp was pulled down off the ceiling. Angela Dawn was the first thing in his life that David could call his own, and she was wrenched from him before she could even say "Daddy".

David returned to Wiles Street, packed the baby's clothes and threw the suitcase down the railway embankment.

Maureen went to stay with her parents in Eaton Street, and David moved back into his grandparents house in Aked Street, where Angela Dawn's body was placed in the front room to await burial.

On the day of the funeral, Myra arrived in the van. Ian remained outside, while she went into the house with a bouquet of flowers. She placed them on a table, took out a pen and wrote a message on the card: ANOTHER LITTLE FLOWER FOR GOD'S GARDEN.

Myra was ashamed of her tears. "Don't tell Ian," she said, and quickly left.

★ ★ ★

Ian Brady knew that he was on the verge of hooking his man.

Over the months he raised the ante with the guns, until one day, strolling on the moors, he revealed to David how far he was willing to go. A shepherd was on the brow of a hill. He had raised his rifle and was focusing on Puppet, who was racing towards the sheep. Would the shepherd fire at the dog? Not if Ian had anything to do with it: he aimed his Smith and Wesson at the shepherd. Suddenly Puppet veered away, the shepherd lowered his rifle, and Ian loosened his grip on the trigger.

Every one of Ian Brady's acts was measured in its intention, but there was one notable exception. Even today, over 20 years later, he rebukes himself for an impetuous act of violence which might have jeopardised his mission in life. It happened as they were driving to Blackpool. A black Ford Popular overtook them, and its driver blew his horn in annoyance. "Someone in the back seat was giving the V sign," recalls Ian.

"I said 'Pass him'. We were cruising along at about 50, at the most. She started to overtake, and as we came abreast I rolled down the window. In the pocket of the car there was a wine bottle. As we came abreast I put my arm right out of the car. I don't know if they put the break on, but the bottle missed them by an inch. I was astonished it didn't hit them. There were about six people packed in this little car."

As they sped on Ian realised that he could have caused a fatal accident. "I remember thinking 'What a stupid thing to do'." No, he was not worried about causing injuries to the occupants. His concern was with his own safety. What if they had taken the registration number of Myra's turquoise blue mini traveller? What if the police had radioed ahead to watch for them as they drove into Blackpool? Ian was angry with himself for an act of indulgence. "It was a sort of madness." He ordered Myra to turn round and return to Manchester. I was thinking in terms of 'Car off the road, what's the best thing to do – go back and make sure there's nobody left'."

Now the time was drawing closer to introduce his pupil David Smith to the sacred texts. His creed was drawn from a hotch-potch of books on fascism and pornography, such as Adolf Hitler's biography and the Marquis de Sade's *Justine*. In their late-night seminars, after the sisters had been despatched to bed, they wrestled with the key planks of Ian's philosophy with the aid of a liberal flow of wine. Smith recorded some of the fragments of wisdom under the heading "Notes from books I have enjoyed, copied for further enjoyment"; statements such as "God is a superstition, a cancer injected into religion . . ." and: "God is a disease, a plague, a weight round a man's neck".

From the noble Marquis: "Rape is not a crime, it is a state of mind, God is a disease which eats away a man's instincts, murder is a hobby and a supreme pleasure".

Ian knew he had triumphed when the youth finally appeared to adopt his pantheism – "Nature is sufficient, and needs no creator" – and abandoned conventional moral standards – "Did not Romulus permit infanticide?"

David did have difficulty in perceiving beauty in the miles of black peat moors, beauty which Ian beheld in his eyes. But he was happy to go along for the wine and target practice with the Webley and Smith and Wesson. His values and critical powers, such as they were, had melted in the onslaught on his senses. Life now was a single hypnotic experience. As if in a trance, the pupil accepted the word of the Master.

"Brady was destructive about religion," he now recalls. "In Nazi Germany, he told me, they didn't allow religion and the country built itself into an industrial power. This was also partly because their unions were not strong. Ian listened to German speeches on his tape recorder, and I was impressed by the way in which he sent for records to be made of Nazi speeches and songs. Ian hated Jews and blacks. I didn't think he was cracked. I thought he was intellectual. I thought he was impressive. His philosophy about Jews and pornography seemed right."

The words embedded themselves in David Smith's mind, and the deeds corroded his soul, until one day the novice was ready to be baptised into the cult. Ian had learnt the secret of immortality, and he was going to share his precious knowledge with David Smith. David now began to think the unthinkable.

CHAPTER ELEVEN

The Missing Murder

David Smith had been out of circulation from his old Gorton haunts for some while, now, and his reputation as a street fighter was suffering. By early 1965, he knew he was in trouble when two youths with whom he was on no more than nodding acquaintance became bold enough to brag about their fights with him. In fact, "I had never raised an eyebrow to them, never mind a fist".

Worse still, however, was the rumour about Sammy Jepson. David and Sammy had been good friends; they had been in some close shaves together, and had stood shoulder-to-shoulder in court when they were convicted of store-breaking. David had gone out with Sammy's sister, Barbara, and he had slept in the Jepson home in Taylor Street. Word was now filtering back that Sammy was claiming in the pubs that he had slept with Maureen. Honour had to be satisfied.

The opportunity presented itself one day as the two friends found themselves walking on the opposite sides of Taylor Street. Sammy was startled to see David race across the road. "I want you," he said, and threw a right punch into his friend's face, cutting his lip and making his nose bleed.

David was unwilling to leave it at that, however, and a short while later he tracked Sammy down to his flat in Longsight. It was late in the evening. Sammy, thicker set than David, was stripped naked to his waist. He was unwilling to get involved in a prolonged knuckle dust-up: he shot out into the road and disappeared into the night.

Sammy was not the only one who was being linked romantically with Maureen, however. Tony Latham, Gloria Molyneux's erstwhile suitor, was also rumoured to have enjoyed Maureen's sexual favours. David did not believe the rumours, but they hurt him; and he was not of a forgetting nature.

* * *

The Smiths occupied a third-floor flat in Underwood Court, 400 yards from Granny Maybury's house. David had refused to return to Wiles Street after the death of his baby, and the council agreed to rehouse him on the new estate in Hattersley. That meant a painful separation from Peggy, the retriever whom he was forced to leave behind in an empty house. Council regulations forbade him from keeping the dog in his apartment.

David's father arranged for the dog to be put down. Myra was distressed to hear the news. She drove to the kennels to rescue the dog: she was too late, it was dead.

David went back into grief. He mixed his drinks, trying to drown his sorrows. Ian and Myra arrived to find him sick in bed. David wanted to be consoled, but Maureen did not seem to be able to help. Ian entered the bedroom and ordered Maureen out. "Leave him to me," he said, and David's spirits immediately rose. David was pleased that his friend had taken command. "I wanted somebody to comfort me, but I didn't want woman's stuff. With Ian there, it was like metal to metal."

Ian shared David's affection for dogs, and he had no doubt about what ought to be done to Smith Senior: "It is that bleeder who should have got the needle, not the dog".

On top of Peggy's demise, David lost his job. Again, Ian came to the rescue: now was the time to get some easy money by robbing a bank. David agreed, and he listened to how Ian had spent years compiling information on "investment establishments" that might one day be relieved of their assets.

They decided to rob the Williams & Glynn's branch in Ashton Old Road. Myra drove David to Manchester and dropped him off near the bank. There, armed with a notebook and the Smith and Wesson – its chambers empty of bullets – David spent three hours noting the comings and goings. Ian had instructed him to record the movement of people who left the premises with large cases.

But Ian was less interested in the detail of what David had written down than in gauging just how far his prospective partner in crime was willing to commit himself.

"How far are you prepared to go?" he asked. "In the event of the robbery, are you prepared to let them have it?" He held up his right hand and went through the actions of squeezing the trigger of a pistol.

He suggested a hypothetical situation. The driver of a security van could alert the police by using his radio. Rather than give him the time which he would have if they tried to smash the windscreen with a pick-axe, was David prepared to shoot the driver?

He was testing the youth with every possible allusion to murder. Time and again he came back to the fundamental question, approaching it from different angles, constantly seeking the kind of firm commitment which would give him confidence in his partner's intentions.

"How do I know you can do it?" he kept asking, once "the girls" had been sent to bed and the wine flowed.

"You don't really understand, do you?" he goaded.

"What's that?" asked David through the haze of alcohol.

Ian finally challenged him with the ultimate question: "Are you capable of murder?"

The cards were now about to be turned face up on the table. It was the point at which David Smith could "bottle out". Ian was at the delicate stage in his brainwashing game, and he had to bolster the lad with courage and reassurances.

"I've done it," he declared. "I have already killed three or four."

David, through bleary eyes, knew that Ian had consumed a large amount of wine. His reaction suggested that he was sceptical, which provoked Ian into further disclosures.

"Don't you believe me? I have photographs to prove it. You and your wife have sat near one of my victims, but I won't tell you where."

The secrets of the moors were slowly being revealed.

They discussed the justifications for murder. David cannot recall the details too clearly, now, beyond his declaration that there was no justification for killing children. Ian acknowledged this reservation, and explained that he always chose people aged between 16 and 20 because their disappearance did not alarm the police.

He had two methods for trapping his victims. "The first one is to wait in a car in a street I have picked out before. I wait for the right moment for someone to walk past, then I get out of the car and murder them."

He did not like this method very much, however, because it entailed a lot of preparation, particularly in relation to the cleaning of his shoes and the car. "For this type of murder I wear a boiler suit over my clothes."

The second method was to lure someone into the car and take them back home to be murdered, after which he buried the bodies on the moors. "I tell you, you've been sitting near where I buried one of the bodies," he insisted.

       ★   ★   ★

Ian Brady was aware that during the course of 1965 he was rapidly losing control of himself. "I felt old at 26. Everything was ashes. I felt there was nothing of interest – nothing to hook myself onto. I had experienced everything." When his life-forces ran flat, he drew his energy from other sources. "You either strike inwards, or you strike outwards, and I was then striking outwards."

But the cold-blooded calculation of the previous years was being replaced by a recklessness that exposed him to potentially fatal mistakes.

David Smith caught a hint of this devil-may-care attitude one night when Ian suggested that they play Russian roulette with a pistol. "I thought he meant with the starting pistol or the air guns that I had in Wiles Street."

Ian was deadly serious, however. He took a revolver from the shoulder holster and extracted the bullets. He placed one back in the pistol, leaving four on the table. He pointed the barrel at David and squeezed the trigger: nothing happened.

"There would have been an awful mess behind you if the bullet hit you," he said with a laugh.

Ian Brady was now ready to make his move.

"Is there anybody you really hate?" he asked.

"Well, there are plenty of people I really hate," replied David.

"But people you *really* hate, that you don't want around?"

Smith paused for a few seconds, then identified the man he hated most: Sammy Jepson. He was at the top of David Smith's list of candidates for murder. His second choice was Tony Latham. Smith then mentioned several other names, and Brady finally stopped him.

"Why do you want them done?" he asked.

"It's to do with Maureen."

"If it's dirty, I don't want to know."

"It's not dirty," David reassured him, "but they've been saying things."

Ian then asked detailed questions about Sammy Jepson – where he lived, the size of his family, and what David knew about him. He then turned his attention to Tony Latham. After a few minutes discussion, Jepson was discarded because he lived in Gorton. Latham was elected as the victim.

"Is it real?" Ian pressed him. "Has it got to you?"

"Of course it's bloody real!"

Latham was big in stature, so Ian would need the advantage of surprise if he was going to kill him. Ian therefore had to pin-point his quarry with care. "I need a photograph."

"I can use my Polaroid camera," David suggested.

The place to photograph Tony was in his favourite pub, the Dolphin in Hyde Road. Ian coaxed his apprentice. "We'll take you down. Keep him talking, make him nice and friendly. Set him up good and proper. Ask him 'Do you drink here often?' Introduce him to the camera like you just happened to have it there, and take a snap of him."

The conspiracy to murder was hatched. It was the middle of the summer, and Ian Brady was ready for his next sacrifice. This time, he would baptise his second disciple into his killing cult.

* * *

David Smith walked across to Wardle Brook Avenue and met Myra and Ian at the van. Over his shoulder was the latest innovation in photographic technology, a Polaroid Land camera that provided instant photographs. In his pocket was a new set of flash bulbs that he had bought for the occasion.

Myra drove along Hyde Road and pulled up at the back of a cinema known locally as The Flea Pit.

Tony Latham was sitting at a table with a group of his friends. He looked up and nodded at David, who was buying a pint of Guinness at the bar. It was Tony's pub, so he did not have to make the running in the social graces. David was the interloper. He walked across to Tony's group, casually placed the camera on the table and sat on one of the stools.

The camera quickly became the focal point of curiosity. "How much was that?" "What are you walking around with that for?" David handed it round for the men to examine, then he peered through the viewfinder and panned around the room until he was looking at his old enemy, Tony Latham. He pressed the button. The shutter made a funny noise, which left David with an apprehensive feeling.

He slipped into the toilets, locked himself in a cubicle and opened the back of the camera to extract the film. Nothing: it was empty. His first major murder assignment and he had blown it! What would Ian say? He will be bloody furious! David caught a bus home, and had a sleepless night. The following evening he sheepishly turned up at Wardle Brook Avenue and confessed to failure. Ian seemed to accept the explanation, but he was concerned about whether Tony Latham suspected their plan. "Does he know anything about it?" he anxiously probed.

Did David Smith seriously intend to cooperate with Ian

Brady in the murder of Tony Latham? Smith's answer now is firm enough: "I wanted him dead, and I went out to buy new flash bulbs specially for that night. I just didn't check to make sure that I had film in the camera.

"On reflection, Latham and Jepson all too easily became a casual matter, fixed as a fact and as important by an all too casual mixture of wine and talk, backed by boozy philosophy – understood, or not, it didn't matter to me: it just sounded right – and the atmosphere topped off by Adolf Hitler ranting away in the background.

"Latham was 'selected' from within this atmosphere, but surely only by name alone? The trip to the Dolphin, the taking of his photo by the time of the next tease, the company, surely the conversation would be different? If not, I don't believe I cared all that much. Latham was left, but in Brady's head it became a proving of himself."

To David Smith, the plot to murder Tony Latham was by now no more significant than the blasting of a sheep on the moors or the rapid-fire annihilation of a bottle of German wine.

To Ian Brady, however, the failure was a catastrophe. The killing of Tony Latham was the test for his protégé. As with the death of Pauline Reade, which hooked Myra, Tony Latham's demise was intended to seal the bonds that would lock Smith to Brady. But now Smith had learnt his secrets and repaid him with failure. He could not countenance failure, and something would have to be done. Smith was now a danger – he knew too much.

CHAPTER TWELVE

The Baptism

Ian Brady was distraught. The rhythm of his life had been disrupted, and David Smith, the man in whom he had vested trust, had failed the blood test. Doubts assailed his mind. "Something was telling me that there was a flaw in him. It was there, gnawing at me." He began to fear that his freedom was now at risk.

He confided his doubts to Myra as they sat in the car high up in the Derbyshire hills near Buxton. Clouds scudded across the evening sky and the lambs frolicked playfully. Life was renewing itself, but the terminal thoughts buried in Brady's mind came to the surface.

"Think it's time he went?"

He did not mention a name, but Myra knew he was talking about her brother-in-law. She sipped her wine, and thought deeply about the proposition. He drew deeply on his cigarette.

Recalling the incident for me, Brady likened it to a Hollywood scene.

"I offered to just kill him, you know, like in a film. We were just sitting, discussing it as if we were discussing some triviality. But it was real."

He was a film buff, but Myra knew that he was not bluffing. She was silent for a few moments. What about Maureen? How would she feel?

"It would hurt Mo."

Maybe, but Ian knew what he would do if it was a choice between Maureen's feelings and Myra's freedom: *Kill David Smith, any day!*

Concealing their responsibility would be a problem, but an opportunity would present itself in time. And it did, within a few weeks. Maureen and David had a row, and she went straight round to Wardle Brook Avenue to ask Myra to drive her to their mum's.

David came round later. "Where's Mo?"

That is when Brady would have seized his chance – if only Myra had not vetoed his proposal!

" 'We'll take you,' " is how he conceived the start of the chain of events. "Head out of Manchester. Take the .38 Smith and Wesson. Blow his head off. Mo some days or weeks later would have enquired if we had heard anything from him. Nothing."

The trail would not have led back to Wardle Brook Avenue. Why should it? Smith was a missing person. Because of his age, the police would not get excited: a matrimonial row, missus walked out on him – not a police matter, sir, he probably took a train to London to make a fresh start.

But Myra was not happy. "It was always Mo this, and Mo that," Brady recalled with irritation. "She didn't want to hurt Mo. Mo baby – you know, she was the younger sister."

Such mundane considerations had no place in his scheme of things. The doubts tormented his mind relentlessly, but Myra cared for her baby sister, and that was that. The girl had to have her way sometimes. Smith would be given one more chance. This time, though, he had better not let them down.

Summer progressed, the days closed in, but the temperatures stayed high. The leaves turned brown, but the rains did not come: autumn was an Indian summer.

The Face of Death needed another sacrifice: one was now months overdue, and the knot was turning tighter in Brady's head.

* * *

On Saturday, September 18, 1965, Brady and Hindley packed their car and headed north. It was their annual holiday, and Ian was on a pilgrimage to the hills of Loch Lomond.

Lunch was sandwiches and a bottle of wine by a stream off the main road south of Carlisle. The green fields rolled away

Above: Ian Brady with classmates. Brady is third from left, back row

Left: Myra Hindley as a schoolgirl

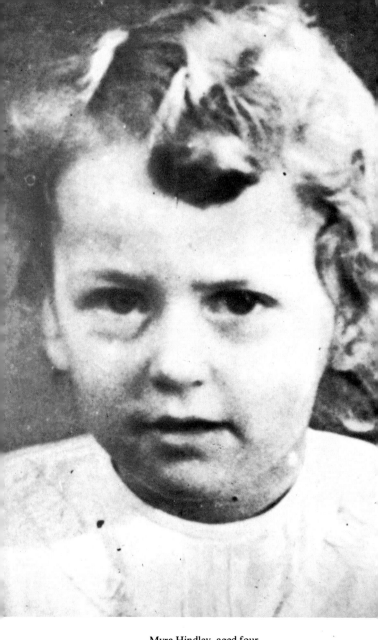

Myra Hindley, aged four

Left: David Smith with his grandmother, Annie Smith

Below: David Smith with his mother, Joyce Hull

Left: Myra Hindley in 1961, the year she met Ian Brady

Below: Ian Brady on his way to court

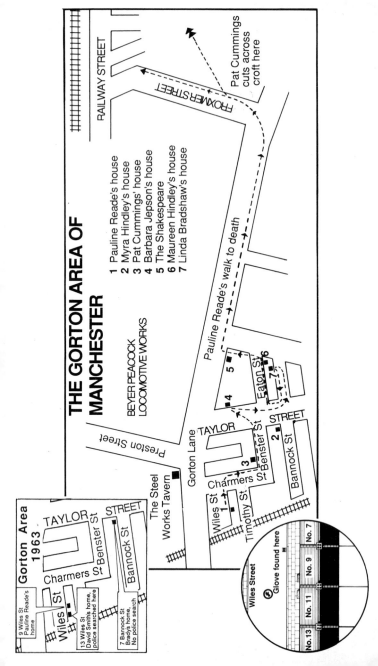

THE GORTON AREA OF MANCHESTER

BEYER PEACOCK LOCOMOTIVE WORKS

1 Pauline Reade's house
2 Myra Hindley's house
3 Pat Cummings' house
4 Barbara Jepson's house
5 The Shakespeare
6 Maureen Hindley's house
7 Linda Bradshaw's house

RAILWAY STREET

FROXMER STREET

Pat Cummings cuts across croft here

Pauline Reade's walk to death

Preston Street

Gorton Lane

TAYLOR STREET

The Steel Works Tavern

Charmers St
Benster St
Bannock St
Wiles St
Timothy St
Eaton St

Gorton Area 1963

TAYLOR STREET
Charmers St
Benster St
Bannock St
Wiles St

9 Wiles St Pauline Reade's home
13 Wiles St, David Smiths home, police searched here
7 Bannock St Bradys home. No police search

Wiles Street

Glove found here

No. 13   No. 11   No. 9   No. 7

Above: Pauline Reade with her brother Paul outside their house in Wiles Street, Gorton

Left: Mrs Joan Reade on the spot where she found Pauline's white glove, outside 9 Wiles Street

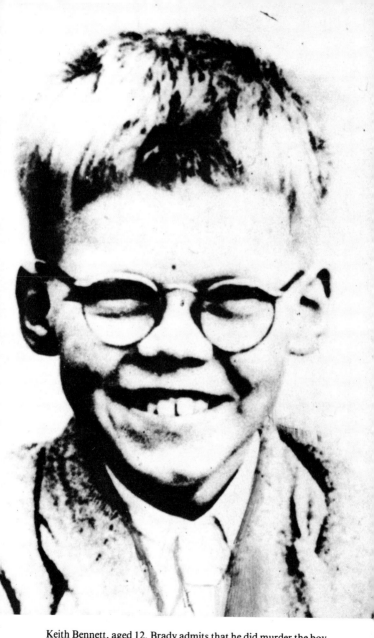

Keith Bennett, aged 12. Brady admits that he did murder the boy and claims that Myra was also involved

Left: Myra Hindley at the time of her arrest

Below: Ian Brady at the time of his arrest

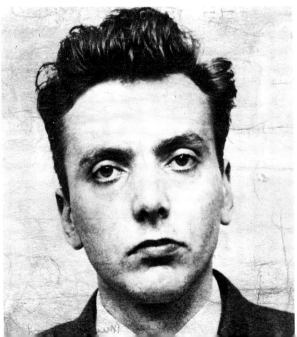

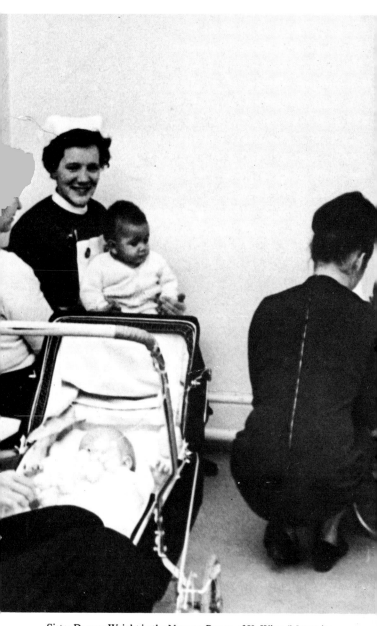

Sister Doreen Wright in the Nursery Room of K. Wing (Maternity quarters), Holloway Prison, with two prisoners and children

Recent picture of Myra Hindley

David Smith, his wife Mary and their daughter Joddy in 1986

David Smith on Saddleworth Moor, on the spot where Brady and Hindley used to picnic

Drawing of Ian Brady in Cell 4, Gartree Prison in 1985.
(Artist: Bob Williams)

Detective Chief Superintendent Peter Topping on Saddleworth Moor

Police with sniffer dogs start the search on the moors for the missing bodies

into the distance. The tensions in Ian's soul dissolved as he lay back to enjoy the tranquillity.

Myra was a little apprehensive. Her lover was going to introduce her to his foster-family, and she wanted to make a good impression. She packed the hamper and they took to the road again. Brady's exhilaration mounted as they drove over the hills. Mile after mile, he soaked in the drystone walls, the gorse-topped hills, flocks of sheep, Myra skilfully negotiating the twisting road as it bore its way over the mountains into Gretna Green and Scotland.

Then, as dusk descended, the glow in the sky above Glasgow. Back into the familiar streets, and all the anxieties flooded back to cast a black cloud on Ian Brady's home-coming. What would the Sloans think of Myra? What would they make of *him*?

No, he would not arrive unannounced at his foster-mother's home. Mrs Sloan was a lovely lady: he recalled her with fondest memories. But it was better that they check into a hotel. He would go ahead, to spy out the lie of the land.

Myra spent an angry evening by herself. Now the doubts returned to her as well. Was he ashamed of her? Why had he never told her that he loved her?

The doubts evaporated when he returned. He had seen his foster-sisters, May and Jean. "I told them that I have a girlfriend, and that I would probably stay with her for the rest of my life," said Ian in one of his rare moments of tenderness.

Myra, when she later recalled that moment, knew that this was the closest her man would ever come to saying "I love you".

The next day, Ian introduced Myra to the family. They were delighted with her. He snapped away with his Japanese camera. She took pleasure in showing them photographs of Puppet.

Ian escorted his girl round some of his old boyhood haunts, and they revisited the hills around Loch Lomond. But the pain deep inside him was returning. It would not be too long, now, before he snapped again. Someone had to die.

★   ★   ★

During the week after his return from Glasgow, Brady made preparations with David Smith to rob the local Electricity Board showroom on October 8. At the same time, however, he could not resist the temptation to hint that the blood test was on the way. It happened in the Smiths' apartment late at night. The sisters went to bed, leaving the men to talk. The subject turned to murder.

According to David's testimony in court, Brady repeated that he had killed on three or four occasions. He then added: "You do not believe I am capable of it, but it will be done. I am not due for another one for three months, and this one won't count".

That last comment – "I am not due for another one for three months, and this one won't count" – has always seemed perplexing. What did he mean? We now know. A death in October would be midway between the ritualised cycle of one death in the summer and another one in winter, around Christmas. Fermenting in Brady's mind was a plot to baptise Smith in blood, but the death would have to be soon – and that meant it could not be synchronised into his established time-table.

But first there was the robbery to get out of the way. Every piece of incriminating evidence had to be cleared out of the house. On Tuesday, October 5, Brady packed two suitcases, one brown, the other blue. David Smith brought his literature wrapped in brown paper to deposit in one of the cases, and he helped Ian to load them into the van.

"Whatever you do, don't drop it or it will blow the lot of us up," he cautioned Myra. Brady and Hindley then drove to Manchester Central, where they handed the cases to the clerk in the left luggage office. They returned home and hid the receipt.

* * *

Late on Thursday afternoon Ian packed away the files in his office at Millwards, joined Myra in the car park, and they drove back to Hattersley. Myra went into the kitchen to prepare tea, while Ian collected Puppet and Lassie and took them down to the valley. He had his camera with him as he left the house. He wanted to finish off the roll with the Glasgow snaps. There were five frames left, and he could take some pictures of the dogs.

As he drew close to Underwood Court, David Smith called him from the balcony. Smith ran down and showed Brady a letter. He was in arrears with his rent to the tune of £14 8s, which meant trouble. Could Ian help? "Leave it to me," said Brady, and he strolled down to the valley, thinking fast.

This was it. The boy needs money, and I have to put him to the test – find out, once and for all, if he is reliable. Brady shot four of the frames of his film and returned briskly to the house.

"Myra," he called as he stood in the garden. "Come out here. I'll take your photo."

Myra straightened her hair and emerged through the back door. Alright, why not get Pat Hodges to pose as well? Myra called Pat who was in her garden at No 12. Pat hurried across and stood next to Myra for the last photograph that Ian ever took.

After tea Brady changed his shirt, slipped on his cuff links, and donned his grey suit, the one with the waistcoat. Myra selected a figure-hugging dress the colour of leopard skin. David Smith was in the house. He had called to borrow a packet of tea from Granny Maybury, but they had few words for him. They were on a mission.

The couple left in their mini Countryman without waving farewell, heading for the centre of Manchester. The purpose of the journey, he told the trial jury, was to "roll a queer" for some rent money for Smith. In fact, as he has now told me, Brady had something more fatal in mind.

Myra drove to Manchester Central and Brady walked to the buffet. It was closed. As he turned he saw a slim-hipped lad in tight jeans and suede jacket standing by the milk-vending machine. Edward Evans was an engineer by trade. Brady had first seen the 17-year-old youth in one of the gay bars some months before. He recognised him tonight as a likely lad for his purpose, and it did not matter how much money he had in his pocket.

"Fancy a drink, Eddie?" he asked. "You can come to my home. My sister's in the car outside. She'll drive us there."

"Aye," said the acne-faced youth, who was ready for a bit of fun after what had been a disappointing evening.

They walked quickly out to the car. "Myra, this is a friend of mine. We are just going back for a drink."

"Hi. Jump in," said Myra.

Edward eased himself into the seat next to the blond, and Ian sat directly behind him. Few words were exchanged in the half-hour it took to drive back to Hattersley.

Once in the house, Eddie was given a drink of wine while Myra popped upstairs to change into something comfortable. "Her killing clothes," as Smith was to call them.

Then Myra nipped across to the tower block with a message for Maureen to give to her mother. "Mo, tell our mam I'll call in tomorrow night for her to bleach me hair."

Maureen was puzzled that her sister had bothered to come across that late at night – almost midnight – for such a trivial reason.

"Dave, see me home through the houses, it's dark and I'm scared," said Myra as she took the handle of the door. David pulled on his jacket, picked up his dog stick and walked briskly across Wardle Brook Walk with his sister-in-law. The Test had begun.

Myra asked David to wait near the wall of the New Inn while she checked if Ian was doing anything. The landing lights flashed on and off three times – the signal: David ran up the slope and into the garden. Ian opened the front door. "Hello, want to see those miniature bottles?" he asked loudly.

David was always game for a swift drink, miniature or otherwise. He waited in the kitchen. Ian disappeared upstairs, and returned with three bottles which he placed on the table. Then he went into the front living room, picked up the axe by the fireplace and brought the blade down on the head of Edward Evans.

A scream, and Myra called "Dave, help him! Help him!"

David ran into the living room and saw his chum Ian crashing blow after blow onto the youth's head. Brady was holding the axe in his right hand. He was bending over, left hand on his knee to steady himself, and he took 14 measured blows with as little passion showing on his face as you would expect from someone chopping wood.

The youth would not lie still. This was not how it happened in the films – that surge of nausea in the stomach as a human being writhed in agony.

"Fuckin' cunt!" swore Brady, as if blaming the boy for forcing him into this murderous act.

"You dirty bastard!"

Methodically, he hacked away like a lumberjack until the bloody pulp collapsed on the floor. Then he smothered the face with a cushion and tied a cord around the neck to stop the gurgling sounds.

Smith stared in disbelief. "He's a gonner." He had drawn blood in his time, and the permanently-splintered bones in his right hand proved it. But this was something else. He could not see any rhyme or reason in it.

David Smith was unaware that the execution was performed exclusively for his benefit. If he had not botched up the Latham conspiracy, Edward Evans would be alive today.

"This is the messiest yet," said Brady to Myra.

The baptism was over. Brady searched Smith's face as he set about swabbing the walls and the top of the door with soapy liquid. Smith and Myra cleaned the floor.

The body was bound up and rolled into a blanket. All the time, Brady scrutinised David Smith through half-closed eyes. He examined the boy's hands closely: they were not shaking.

"Eddie's a dead weight," quipped Ian as they carried him upstairs and dumped him in a bedroom.

Brady went to bed well satisfied with his night's work. Welcome, David Smith, Disciple.

PART FOUR

Confession

CHAPTER THIRTEEN

The Trial

Robert Talbot, the superintendent of Stalybridge Police, wanted to retain the element of surprise. Young David Smith's story about guns in No. 16 Wardle Brook Avenue suggested the need for extreme caution.

He did not have a warrant in his pocket as he cruised into the Hattersley estate around 8 a.m.; but then, he did not need one. He had adequate cause to believe that a crime – murder – might have been committed.

The baker was on his rounds. His van was parked round the corner. Talbot borrowed the baker's white coat. Hiding behind the van, he slipped the coat over his blue tunic and picked up the bread-basket. Twenty five constables formed themselves into a cordon round the terrace. The police chief knew that Brady left for work by 8.20 a.m. That would be the time to arrest him, well away from his guns. The minutes ticked by, and there was no sign of movement from the house. Time for action.

He approached with Det. Sgt. Alexander Carr and knocked on the back door.

"I am a police superintendent," he said, opening the white coat to reveal his uniform.

"Is your husband in?"

"I haven't got a husband," replied Myra.

"I have reason to believe there is a man in this house." Myra Hindley hesitated. Which man was the "Super" referring to? There were two men in the house, and one of them was trussed up like a chicken in the upstairs bedroom, dead as could be.

"There is no man here," she replied emphatically.

"I am not satisfied. I want to come in." And he did, taking the first step into the house of secrets.

Ian Brady was in the living room, lying on the divan bed dressed only in a vest. He was writing a note to his employer, to explain that he could not report for work because he had injured his ankle.

He heard the knock at the back door, but there was nothing to alert him to danger as he scrawled green ink on the notepaper with his ballpoint pen. A 60 second warning was all that he needed to get up the stairs. The two pistols, each with five rounds in the chamber, were locked in the back bedroom. He would not have given himself up willingly: better to have a shoot-out than spend your life in prison.

Too late. Into the living room strode the commanding figure of Superintendent Talbot. There was no visible trace of dried blood. The budgie chirped cheerily in its cage. "What's your name?" asked Talbot.

"Ian Brady."

"I have received a report that an act of violence took place in this house last night, and we are investigating it," explained the officer.

Despite the initial protests from Myra Hindley, he searched the house. Upstairs, Granny Maybury was still in her room, but the rear bedroom was locked. No, he could not have the key. "It is at work," said Myra firmly.

"Alright, get your coat. We will take you to work in the car and bring you back," offered Mr Talbot.

"I do not want to go. It is not convenient," insisted Myra.

She searched her lover's face, which was impassive. "You had better tell him," she said.

"There was a row last night," he began to explain. Then he broke the impasse. "Give them the key."

In the room, the superintendent found the body of the youth. A leg was sticking out of the blanket wrapping. The hatchet was in a brown carrier bag on the floor, near Smith's stick. And the two pistols, their blank chambers facing the trigger pin, were in a cardboard box at the foot of the bed.

Ian Brady was escorted to Hyde police station. He was already one month late in returning his books to the Longsight library, where his fines notched up to 4s 3d. A librarian sent a postcard reminding him to return the books, but it was sent back marked "Gone Away". Ian Brady was never to return.

* * *

For five precious days after Brady's arrest, the police allowed Myra Hindley to walk free. She made occasional visits to the police station, where she stonewalled during interviews. She would not say anything until she had spoken to Ian, and besides, she insisted, her story was the same as Ian's. Before she was arrested on October 11, she destroyed incriminating evidence.[1] But she could not get back into the house in Wardle Brook Avenue, for this was still being examined by the forensic experts.

Within the next few days, Talbot was joined by Det. Chief Supt. Arthur Benfield, the head of Cheshire CID, Chief Inspector Joe Mounsey, from Ashton-under-Lyne, and Det. Chief Inspector John Tyrrell of Manchester. The net was now expanding, for it was beginning to dawn on the police that they had stumbled onto something bigger than an intemperate homicide. The files of missing children were gathered up, sifted, and a list of twelve names was finally assembled for examination.

A Home Office pathologist, Dr. Charles St. Hill, joined detectives in identifying the blood found on garments and objects such as David Smith's dog stick.

Although Smith reported Brady's boast – that he had killed three or four people – the detectives had no solid evidence until Mr Tyrrell decided to have another go at the end-of-terrace house. It was always possible that *something* had been missed during the previous inch-by-inch searches. He picked Myra's

---

[1] Brady made this claim to the author, but he refused to disclose the nature of the evidence which Hindley destroyed.

ivory and gilt bible off the bookshelf. It was inscribed "To Myra from Auntie Kath and Uncle Bert. Souvenir of your first Holy Communion". He flicked through it and discovered, concealed in the spine of the bible, a ticket from Manchester's Central Station. The two cases that were claimed from the left luggage office were as explosive as a ton of gelignite.

Amongst the contents were photographs of Myra standing on Saddleworth Moor, her puppy wrapped inside her jacket for protection against the howling wind. The rambling search of the desolate hillsides off the A635, hampered as the late heatwave gave way to seasonal rainstorms, now assumed cartographic precision. As distressed mothers came to survey the wild scenery, praying that their fears would not be realised, the co-ordinates of Myra's position in relation to the major topographical features – clumps of rocks, mountain peaks – were plotted. These finally established the location of two bodies: those of John Kilbride and Lesley Ann Downey.

Ian Brady, peering through his viewfinder, had placed Myra in the centre of the frame. An innocent enough pose, but in his mind's eye he could see the prostrate body of a child buried inches beneath his lover's feet.

Other photographs were entirely devoid of innocence. They revealed how Brady and Hindley had defiled the bound, gagged and naked body of Lesley Ann Downey in their home in Wardle Brook Ave.

David Smith was singing like a canary. He told the detectives about the late-night drinking sessions, the tutorials in fascist philosophy, and of Brady's account of the best methods of laying in wait for a victim to murder.

He even told them about his conspiracy to murder Anthony Latham, but a decision was made not to proceed with a charge: the prosecution needed the youth as their star witness. Smith, after all, was their primary source of information. He was the expert on the killers who now languished behind bars, neither of whom was being helpful.

Mr Benfield asked Smith if he knew a way of rattling Brady; one mistake might lead to a confession. The question was a serious one; investigators have to use any trick in the book, providing it is within the law. But they were not ready for the ideas that popped out of Smith's head.

The first one was to send a spider into Brady's cell. Smith had seen Ian recoil in terror when a spider – "all legs and no body" – crawled along the living room floor in Wardle Brook Avenue. He raised his knees to remove his feet from danger and ordered Myra to kill it. The idea of releasing a creepy crawly into Brady's cell was probably the only moment of fleeting humour in the weeks of painstaking investigation.

Smith's second suggestion, however, was not amusing. He knew that Myra loved Puppet deeply, so his fertile mind came up with what he thought was a sure-fire way of upsetting Hindley: kill the dog. That would rattle her.[2]

The police regarded this as a callous suggestion, which they rejected. But by one of those strange twists of fate, Myra's love for Puppet was put to the test. For in preparing their case, the police decided to obtain an expert's assessment of Puppet's age. This was because the dog appeared on the photograph that led the detectives to John Kilbride's shallow grave on October 21. Was it taken before or after the burial?

Brady was shown the photograph by Mr Mounsey, and he declared: "It's on the moors somewhere. I took it about eighteen months ago."

Brady was asked how he knew it was taken then. He replied: "The reason I said eighteen months ago is the age of the dog. It is approximately eighteen months old."

To cover his tracks, Brady should have suggested that the photograph was taken two or three years previously – well before John Kilbride had disappeared from his home. Then, he could have argued that it was nothing more than an astonishing coincidence that he had asked Myra to pose near some rocks for a photograph – the spot which was subsequently used by someone else to bury John Kilbride. In that case, of course, it

[2] David Smith disclosed this proposal to the author during an interview on July 26, 1985.

would have helped the prosecution if it could prove that Brady's claim was a lie because based on the dog's approximate date of birth, the photograph had to be taken either about the time of the boy's disappearance, or after.

As it happens, however, Brady even went on to admit that he knew he was taking a photograph of John Kilbride's grave, although he denied that either he or Myra had killed the boy. The admission was enough for the prosecution to mount a charge of murder.

The police decided that it was necessary to present expert testimony on the dog's age.[3] They arranged for the dog to be examined, and Puppet's age was established as between eighteen months and three years. At the committal proceeding the magistrates were told that the dog stopped breathing while under anaesthetic. Artificial respiration was applied for three quarters of an hour, but the dog failed to revive.

Puppet died on November 1. Two police officers drove to Risley, where Brady and Hindley were on remand. They broke the news to the dog's mistress. She is reported to have said: "You police are nothing but murderers". Hindley was livid, but she did not break down and confess.[4]

* * *

Risley, the remand centre for prisoners who are innocent until

---

[3] Emlyn Williams, in his account of the dog's death, states: "It was most important to prove that the photo of Myra on the Kilbride grave had been taken after the boy's disappearance and not before, by establishing that Puppet had been born round about that date, or after". *op. cit.*, p.340.

[4] During the trial, the following exchange occurred between Ian Brady and the Attorney General:

BRADY, referring to an interview with Joe Mounsey, said: "He told me, 'I don't think you have any feelings at all. The only one is for your dog. We will destroy the dog then you will know what it feels like to lose something you love'. And it was destroyed one week later".

ATTORNEY GENERAL: "It is a wicked suggestion that the dog was

proven guilty, is five miles from Warrington, in Cheshire. The view through the windows is of green lawns rather than a concrete exercise yard. It was here that Ian Brady's love for Myra Hindley was put to one of its severest tests. During one of his exercise periods, two prisoners escaped.

"All they did was run to the fence, what we called the privacy fence, which separates the exercise yard behind the hospital from the wall. The wall was not a high one.

"They got to the fence, climbed up it, chucked blankets over the barbed wire, rolled over it and got away. They were gone.

"I don't know whether they were eventually caught, but they got away. And that was in daylight."

The idea that escape was practical was already in Brady's mind. While in custody in Hyde police station, he was escorted by two policemen to the canteen, where he was offered the opportunity to shave. It was a Sunday morning, and the station was otherwise deserted. One officer disappeared, and the second one left Brady alone to deal with a call on the telephone switchboard. Brady noticed that the ground floor canteen had an unbarred window. "I could have stepped into the parking lot, and got away," he told me.

His second opportunity to escape, this time in Risley, came when he was ordered to report to the women's section for an interview with his solicitor.

"They came to take me over, and there were no handcuffs, no walkie-talkies, no police dogs or television cameras.

"There was a pea-soup fog, which was so bad that we were bumping into parked cars. You couldn't even see the beams from the searchlights.

"All I had to do was one step forwards, one step sideways, and that was that. It was a cinch."

deliberately put to death, Brady, and you know it".
BRADY: "It is a funny coincidence".
On October 20, 1985, John Tyrrell, now retired to a South Wales village, informed the author that Smith did refer to Puppet in the context of Brady's love for the dog.

It was now or never, but Brady could not do it; he was not going to abandon "the girl". He had an even greater challenge than a barbed wire fence: to try and persuade a British jury that Myra Hindley was not guilty of the murder of three young people.

As solicitors prepared the defence, a relative of one of the victims made preparations of his own. Patrick Downey, Lesley Ann's uncle, bought a .32 Webley and Scott pistol. He planned a summary execution in the well of the court.

This plan would have brought a sardonic smile onto Brady's face if he had known about it. For one of his favourite passages by the Mad Marquis pronounced:

> Should a murderer be punished by murder? Undoubtedly not. The only punishment which a murderer should be condemned to is that which he risks from the friends or the family of the man he has killed. In a word, murder is a horror but a horror often necessary, never criminal, and essential to tolerate in a republic.[5]

But the police discovered the plot. They cautioned Patrick Downey against taking the law into his own hands.

The accused appeared in court in Chester Castle on April 19, 1966, to answer the charge that they murdered Lesley Ann Downey, John Kilbride and Edward Evans.

Myra, aged 23, her hair freshly dyed in a metallic silver-grey, cut short and with a fringe, wore a grey tweed suit. Ian, aged 28, wore a grey suit with a white handkerchief in the breast pocket, a green tie and a grey check shirt. Together, they huddled in the dock, their backs protected from the public gallery by a shatter-proof glass screen, making copious notes and whispering instructions to their lawyers.

[5] Geoffrey Gorer, *The Life and Ideas of the Marquis de Sade*, p. 140.

What was billed as The Trial of the Century was on, but as far as Brady was concerned his conviction was a foregone conclusion. His sole objective was to try and exonerate Myra Hindley. Nine hundred years of legal precedents were brought into play to ensure that the killers received a fair trial, their innocence presumed until the final second when the jury returned with their verdicts. Slowly, methodically, the prosecution unfolded its case, paraded the exhibits, and sanitized the emotion out of the proceedings. The judge, Mr Justice Fenton Atkinson, noting that the case had attracted immense Press publicity, was satisfied that he had presided over a ritual that accorded with appropriate decorum:

> Happily, inside this court at least, we have been able to avoid any unnecessary sensations and do our best, our job, in trying to see as far as we can the accused have a fair trial and a just verdict.

The due process of law had certainly anaesthetized the players in the drama. The one incident that shattered the calm remains firmly fixed in the memories of the people of Britain to this day: the tape recording of the torture of Lesley Ann Downey. People recall the extracts of the child screaming in pain and pleading for mercy.

Child: "Can I tell you summat? I must tell you summat. Please take your hands off me a minute, please. Please mum, please – I cannot tell you: I cannot breathe . . . Please God . . . Why? What are you going to do with me."

Man: "I want to take some photographs, that is all."

Child: "I want to see my mummy . . . Honest to God. I will swear on the Bible . . . I have got to go because I am going out with my mamma. Please, please help me, will you?"

Man: "The longer it takes you to do this the longer it takes you to get home."

For sixteen relentless minutes the child pleads in desperation.

Child: "It hurts me neck."

Man: "Put it in your mouth and you'll be all right."

Woman: "Shut up crying."

Child (crying): "It hurts me!"

Woman: "Hush. Shut up now. Put it in and don't dally. Just keep your mouth shut, please."

During the police interrogation, Myra Hindley was played that tape. She listened to it with her head bowed, and she sobbed. "I am ashamed," she said. Those few tears were the only signs of remorse that the detectives witnessed from her.

Ashamed she may have been, but Myra Hindley conspired with Brady to try and cast a veil of innocence over her role in the sadism and murders. Brady attempted to accept all the blame for those actions which – in the light of the evidence placed by the prosecution before the court – he could not deny. During the nine hours of cross-examination, not once did he acknowledge Hindley's culpability. He even took full responsibility for putting the gag into Lesley Ann Downey's mouth.

"Who was it gagged the child, you or Hindley?" asked the Attorney General. "Me," replied Brady.

"Did Hindley have any part in gagging the child or trying to gag the child?" "No. I put the handkerchief in Lesley's mouth and put the scarf on, partly to hold the handkerchief in and partly to hide her face to hide her identity."

But talking to her friend Rena Duffy 19 years later, Hindley acknowledged that she had "put a handkerchief in the child's mouth to stop her screaming and crying". The walls of the council house were thin, and she was frightened that the neighbours would hear the girl crying. But Hindley was still adamant: "Emotionally, the child had been damaged, but physically she hadn't".

She continued to maintain, along with Brady's original version, that Lesley Ann Downey was taken away from the photographic session by David Smith. The members of the jury, however, chose to believe Smith. They took two hours 23 minutes to find Brady guilty of all three murders. Hindley was found guilty of two murders, and convicted of harbouring

Brady, knowing that he had killed John Kilbride.

Their life in prison had begun.

* * *

I asked Brady why he did not plead insanity, or at least diminished responsibility. He had considered that possibility, but quickly dismissed it.

"I wanted to help the girl," he says simply. "All my evidence was to get her off." He faltered once only in that determination. The idea came to him when his mother brought him jam in a glass jar. For the first time, he toyed with the idea of suicide.

He told Myra of his plan when he met her during the committal proceedings at Hyde magistrates court. "I really became upset and begged him not to do it," she now recalls. He had found borstal tough to take, and the prospect of life in prison was beginning to weigh heavily on him. But Myra's plea was enough to persuade him to abandon the idea.

Besides, there was still a lot of laughing to do. Ironically, it was the notion of insanity that relieved the tension of those weeks sitting in his cell in Risley.

He borrowed Joseph Heller's novel *Catch 22* from the library. It is a story about bomber pilots and their crews during the Second World War. Uppermost in their minds was the need to escape further bombing missions over enemy territory, in order to avoid becoming casualties. Ian Brady laughed heartily as he read how Yossarian wrestled with the rules.

"Can't you ground someone who's crazy?" he asked Doc Daneeka.

"Oh, sure. I have to. There's a rule saying I have to ground someone who's crazy," admitted the squadron's doctor.

Brady found the catch hilarious: anyone who wants to escape from combat duty isn't really crazy. He recited for me the passage that made the prison wing resound with his laughter:

"There was only one catch and that was Catch-22, which specified that a concern for one's own safety in the face of dangers that were real and immediate was the process of a

rational mind. Orr was crazy and could be grounded. All he
had to do was ask; and as soon as he did, he would no longer be
crazy and would have to fly more missions. Orr would be crazy
to fly more missions and sane if he didn't, but if he was sane he
had to fly them. If he flew then he was crazy and didn't have to;
but if he didn't want to he was sane and had to. Yossarian was
moved very deeply by the absolute simplicity of this clause of
Catch-22 and let out a respectful whistle.

" 'That's some catch, that Catch-22,' he observed.

" 'It's the best there is,' Doc Daneeka agreed."[6]

Brady told me: "I wasn't worried about the trial. I was
relaxed, but it didn't sound too good, me laughing away while
waiting for a trial of murder". He has since read the book twice
more. "I heard the film wasn't very good."

A similar catch faces a guilty person who is being tried for a
serious crime. If he exercises his right to remain silent and not
go into the witness box, he runs the risk of colouring the jury's
mind: they might think that he is guilty; but if he *does* give
evidence, he takes the risk of making damaging admissions
under cross-examination.

No such quandry faced Brady. He confidently – arrogantly –
answered questions for eight and three-quarter hours. He
invited me to "comprehend the whole fabric of the trial". By
that, he meant that he had readily to agree with some points of
the evidence, in order to try and destroy those bits which
implicated Myra.

"I was trying to get her off," he noted time and again. "In
order to maintain this precarious balance I was reinforcing
some things, by saying 'Yeh, that's right', and on other things I
was going out of my way to be destructive with the
prosecution."

In the event, he was rewarded in some small measure. Brady
still derives satisfaction from the fact that he helped Myra to
beat the Kilbride murder charge.

That was not enough for Hindley, however. She appealed

[6] Joseph Heller, *Catch 22*, London: Cape, 1962, pp.45-46.

against the conviction on the grounds that the judge had been wrong to hear the charges against both of them at the same time; that there was a risk that she would be found guilty by her association with Brady. The Lord Chief Justice was not impressed. He pointed out that Brady had at all times sought to exonerate her from any part in his activities. To that extent it was a benefit for her to be tried with Brady[7].

The mayhem that was created by Brady and Hindley stemmed from their indivisible association. That they should be condemned together by the same court was just, for this was the affirmation of the supremacy of those universal values from which no man or woman, no matter how corrupt, can hope to escape. The separation of the lovers was, in fact, the ritual destruction of evil incarnate.

[7] 'Moors Murder Plea Fails', *The Times*, October 18, 1966.

CHAPTER FOURTEEN

Spirits Apart

They escaped with their lives, but something died when they were parted. The Murder (Abolition of Death Penalty) Act 1965 came into force one month after Brady's arrest. By the time justice had been dispensed they could only be sentenced to life in prison. But that was enough to break the blood bond. Ian was sent north to Durham and Myra was transported to Holloway.

For Myra, the drive south was the first stage in the journey to recovery from madness. All she needed was quarantine. It could not be so easy for Ian, however, because he was the source of the infection. He needed skilled treatment in the appropriate environment, but this was denied him because he was deemed to be sane. He opted for solitary confinement under Rule 43 of the prison regulations, which is the safety net for sex offenders and particularly child molesters who are special targets for the dispensation of private justice by the criminal fraternity.

With nothing but time on his hands, now, Ian studied the German language, in which he obtained a GCE at 'O' level. He could not elude the detectives, however, who within a year were knocking on his cell door to find out if he would confess to the murders of Pauline Reade and Keith Bennett. He maintained a morose silence.

He began a strenuous campaign for visiting rights for Myra Hindley. Myra appealed to Lord Longford for help in representing their cause to the Home Office. The lovers argued that, because they were betrothed under common law, they should enjoy the same rights as prisoners who were legally married. Brady needed the personal contact, no matter how tenuous, if he was going to nourish his hold over Myra. Theirs had been a special relationship in which few words were needed to communicate thoughts. "A meshing into one took place" is how Ian now explains what happened when they met. "We didn't need to speak. Just a gesture – something had got to be done, something would happen. I'd just look, or just make a gesture with my hand, and the thing would happen, you know. It was so close, we knew exactly what was in each other's mind. We were one mind."

The Home Office denied the requests, and in 1969 Ian went on the first of a series of hunger strikes. To fill the void in his life, Brady learnt to use a braille machine so that he could produce typescripts for the blind.

The "one mind" had become two again, and officialdom was determined to keep it that way. So Ian and Myra had to settle for a constant flow of letters. Some of their messages were in code. Of one thing they had no doubt: David Smith ought to have been "blown away" in the summer of '65. According to Ian, Myra now agreed. "She said in her letters 'Yes, you should have done it'," he told me.

Intuitively, he knew that the passage of time weakened the prospects of their remaining united in spirit. As the psychiatrists put it:

> The prognosis is usually excellent in those cases where the syndrome has arisen almost entirely from psychological isolation or from psychological contagion with a closely associated primary source, as in *Folie à Deux* – that is, if the isolation can be broken and the primary source removed.[1]

The Brady-Hindley relationship was a paradigm. Ian sucked Myra into his web, isolated her from normal social contact and infected her with his madness. The steel bars smashed the psychological cobwebs that shrouded her mind. Ian could not exercise his thought transference over 260 miles. They began to

[1] Slater and Roth, *op. cit.*, p. 153.

draw apart. Lord Longford witnessed the process of estrangement. He recorded in his autobiography:

> For many months she hesitated to send word to Ian Brady that the old relationship was over, although she would never cease to wish him well. She was aware that her new attitude could easily be misunderstood by him and by others. It was all too obviously in her own interest in a worldly sense to break the connection.[2]

Ian first detected the loosening of the bond through her gradual reconversion to Catholicism. He fought back, sending her barbed comments like "What colour hairshirt are you wearing?" and "What's the penance of the day?" But his inane refutations of religion – such as: "Is heaven filled only with Catholic souls – what about 5m Chinese souls?" – could no longer sway Myra.

"I knocked him off his shrine," is how she now explains it.

But the break was a slow one. "I was frightened to finish with him. He had been such a big part of my life." She dropped hints. One of them was in the form of a Wordsworth poem, which dealt with the transformation of love from passion to maturity. Ian got the message.

* * *

The early years of solitude also had their effect on Ian Brady. He is a man who finds it impossible to say "I am sorry". He began to feel remorse, but his undemonstrative nature prevented him from saying anything public that could be misconstrued, or which could be interpreted as cheap theatrical exhibitionism.

At one stage he contemplated donating a kidney as an act that would help to "balance the past".[3] And he indicated to me

[2] Longford, *op. cit.*, p. 141.
[3] *ibid.*, p. 145.

that his work for the blind, in the privacy of his cell, was a positive expression of his sorrow. "Action, not words," was his way of conveying his feelings.

"I'm not interested in verbal hairshirts, sack-cloth and ashes," he told me. "I'm not interested in people expressing remorse, because even they don't know where the line stops between remorse for being caught or remorse for the act. They don't know, they just play a role. They play that role for so many years that they become the role. M's a good case."

So to discern how the full horror of his cold-blooded killings was unconsciously gnawing away at his mind, we have to identify the visible signals. One of these was the explosion when he came face-to-face with Raymond Morris on December 12, 1969.

Morris was convicted of the murder of seven-year-old Christine Darby in 1967. Like Brady, Morris used a camera to take pornographic photographs of children whom he kidnapped in the streets. Like Brady, he hid Christine's body in the countryside after sexually abusing her in a coppice on Cannock Chase, in the West Midlands. As with Brady, the police wanted to know if Morris was connected with the disappearance of other children.[4] On the surface, at any rate, there was little to choose between the two men: they were mirror images of each other.

None of this went through Ian Brady's mind as he poured himself a cup of tea from an urn in the TV room in Durham. But as Morris walked through the door Brady swung his cup and poured the scalding liquid over him. Brady was punished with 28 days confinement in his cell.

On another occasion, he saw Morris coming up some stairs. Brady punched him back down the flight. "I kept after him," he told me. "Three times at Durham, and then I got him again

[4] West Midlands police hold open files on Margaret Reynolds, aged 6, of Birmingham, and Diane Tift, aged 5, of Bloxwich, Staffordshire, whose bodies were found 300 yeards from each other in a ditch on Cannock Chase in January 1966. This case is documented by Harry Hawkes in *Murder on the A 34*, London: John Long, 1970.

at Albany. Years later, during a calm period in the Scrubbs, I realised that, in a way, I was attacking myself. I could see a reflection of me in the Cannock Chase killer." A reflection that he was growing to dislike.

* * *

David Smith was suffering as well. Despite his decision to report Ian for the murder of Edward Evans, and his resolute testimony that helped the jury to convict his friend of three murders, the citizens of Manchester decided that he must have been more deeply involved in the Moors murders. So, exercising their utilitarian right to ostracise him, they began to exact retribution without needing to establish that he was guilty.

Maureen, now aged 20, gave birth to their first son in May 1966. David could not support his family, however, because no-one would employ him. When he did finally secure a job, the other employees threatened to walk out of the factory unless he was immediately dismissed. David was sacked before he had completed his first day's work. The same thing happened when he found another job two days later.

Verbal abuse and fist-fights became routine as angry (and occasionally drunk) neighbours in Hattersley articulated their feelings. By 1969 Smith had had enough. In a frenzy he repeatedly stabbed a neighbour, William Lees, and found himself standing in the same dock once occupied by Ian Brady and Myra Hindley. The judge, Mr Justice Veale, said he accepted that since the Moors trial David had been "subjected to a great deal of open and sustained hostility". Nonetheless, a prison sentence of three years was deemed to be appropriate in the light of his four previous convictions for assault.

"Lees copped it for 15 years of frustration," is how David now recalls that incident. "He copped it for Angela Dawn, for my mum, the death of Peggy, the Moors trial – everything.

"The week before I knifed Lees, he and a few others had gone for me. They gripped me and held me in the road. Cars were swerving as women were kicking me with their stiletto heels. A week later, while I was on bail for stabbing someone, Lees & Co gave me a good hiding. I took it, and didn't complain to the police. A few days later I was in a nigger's house, having a bit of a relationship with him and his wife, and Lees came into the house and starts thumping me. I picked up a knife and striped him across the face.''

Like Ian Brady, David Smith opted for Rule 43. Prison, he now acknowledges, worked wonders for him. "It took me out of circulation and allowed me just enough time to think about everything that had happened to me. I needed that time. I literally slowed down.'' When he came out, he felt that he was a changed man. In the meantime, Maureen felt that she wanted a change of lifestyle too: she walked out on him and abandoned their three sons.

David soon had another brush with the law, however. In 1972 he administered an overdose of sleeping tablets to his father, who was suffering from cancer. The police charged him with murder, but the court found him guilty of manslaughter. The judge dismissed him with a nominal two-day prison sentence.

CHAPTER FIFTEEN

Parable of Mektoub

Separation from Ian Brady was not enough. New relationships were vital if Myra Hindley was to recover from the nightmare that she helped to create and which, in the end, devoured her. The early years in prison were filled with defiance and malice, but she slowly mellowed in response to the advances from her jailers and some of the inmates.

The turning point in her return to normality was probably 1972. By then she had spent seven years away from Ian, long enough for her to establish new bearings. In that year, on September 12, the Governor of Holloway, Mrs Dorothy Wing, took a calculated risk by escorting Myra on a 90-minute stroll on Hampstead Heath. When it became public knowledge, that gesture provoked a fierce outcry of indignation. But an important lesson was not lost on Myra: now she *knew* that some people had faith in her.

The path was not straight and narrow, however, for she established a lesbian relationship with a prison officer, Patricia Cairns; together they plotted an escape which ended in a court appearance. Myra was given a one-year sentence and Cairns was sentenced to six years in prison.

After this she settled down to a diligent routine that was punctuated by attacks on her by unsympathetic inmates. The bleach blond reverted to natural brown hair. Myra was courteous to the staff and helpful to new inmates who needed to be shown the ropes of life in prison. She embarked on a course of studies which in 1980 earned her a BA Honours degree in the Humanities from the Open University.

The world suspected her motives. Was she really a reformed character, or was she playing the system for what it was worth –

parole? She did long for her freedom, but she remained steadfast in her claim that she was largely innocent of her former lover's evil crimes. Lord Longford zealously represented her cause in Whitehall and in the media, and one day Myra sat down to pen what she presented as a comprehensive account of her deeds. This 20,000-word document turned Ian Brady into her deadliest enemy.

* * *

Ian Brady, shuttling between Parkhurst and Albany prisons, on the Isle of Wight, was furious. Myra's document, while it may not have been a complete and honest disclosure of her role, deviated from the story that he had fabricated for her at the trial.

The damage that was inflicted on the relationship between the former lovers was irreparable. This placed Lord Longford in an awkward predicament, for he had befriended both of them. Longford knew that Myra's prospects of parole would be enhanced if the Parole Board could be convinced that hers had been a subservient role. So the Labour peer, on one of his visits to Wormwood Scrubbs, asked Ian if he would reaffirm the account of Myra's role that he had delivered at the trial. That account, of course, was a white-wash, in which Ian perjured himself as an expression of his commitment to Myra. He bluntly refused to co-operate, and he later told me why by reciting a Turkish parable, the Parable of Mektoub.

Mektoub, as Ian Brady recounted it, was a master of the martial arts. He tutored one of his pupils in over 300 moves that were designed to overcome an opponent. One day, master and pupil faced each other in a tournament. The master overwhelmed his pupil with a swift move. The pupil was taken unawares; he could not anticipate the move because the master had failed to teach it to him. The master, it appears, had kept that one move up his sleeve, to ensure that he retained the upper hand in case he should find himself in combat with his pupil.

Ian Brady was the master, and he had kept one move up his sleeve: he knew the full truth about Myra's role in the moors murders, and by revealing new details he could keep her in prison.

"She must stick to what I created for her defence at the trial, because if she doesn't she'll go down with me," he explained to me.

HARRISON: You told me she betrayed you by giving away some details.
BRADY: She started to elaborate on it in a very subtle way. In other words, she began expanding the image that I had created at the trial.
HARRISON: Of innocence, you mean?
BRADY: Yeh.
HARRISON: Isn't that a logical thing for her to do?
BRADY: Yes, but in such a way that it was including derogatory, shall we say, remarks about me. Like: it gave her a chill to think she might have been in the same cell that I'd been in, in Durham, and things like that.

Ian was particularly furious because he was trying to shake off the Category A status, which restricted his movements within the prison.

BRADY: I mean, for Christ's sake, I gave her the cover and she takes the cover and starts inventing on it. Starts embroidering on it. At my expense. And I gave her it.
HARRISON: It must have been the only thing she thought she could do to help her with the parole.
BRADY: Exactly. She'd come to the stage where she'd do anything to get parole.
HARRISON: It couldn't hurt you, could it, because you didn't want to be let out at any time anyway?
BRADY: I was trying to get off Cat. A, then.

He was acutely sensitive to the hostile public attitude towards them, and of the political implications that flowed from an application for parole. So he was annoyed with Myra for launching a campaign for parole after only seven years in prison. The ensuing publicity was "another drag anchor" on him. "She should have just sat back, kept quiet, waited, made no noise, and she would perhaps have made it after 10, 12 [years]."

Did he now regret not taking his chance to escape from Risley remand centre? "As far as I was concerned, there was no question about it: I was doing the right thing. So I wasn't making any sacrifice."

Now that she had "fictionalised" the account of innocence that he had provided for her, Ian was determined to make sure that she stayed behind bars. "That's the Catch 22. She must stick to what I created for her defence at the trial because if she doesn't she'll go down with me." He does not believe that she should be released from prison, and if there was a realistic prospect of her receiving parole he would release information through his solicitor that would keep her in prison "for another 100 years".

Without any emotion in his voice he said of his former lover: "She's on her own, now". Not entirely. Wherever she walks, his shadow follows her.

* * *

Because of the public antipathy towards the Moors murderers, every development in Myra's case generates a spate of Press publicity. She is the most reviled woman in the British penal system and she has to contend with a sustained media campaign against her, which has a measurable impact on political attitudes and therefore on her prospects for parole.

In 1978, for example, Myra Hindley had served 12 years in prison – the usual length of time for murderers in Britain. She expected to be granted parole, assuming that the Parole Board accepted that she was no longer a danger to children. Unfortunately for Myra, however, an opinion poll conducted by Opinion Research Centre found that 93% of the British public felt that she should not be released. People in the sample were asked for their attitude towards her release if they could be convinced that she was reformed. Sixty-seven per cent said it would still not be right to release her.

Such an overwhelming feeling of animosity could not be ignored by a Home Secretary, who has to take the final decision on whether to parole a murderer. Even the Parole Board itself, though not required to do so, reaches its recommendations by taking public opinion into account. The odds were heavily stacked against Myra Hindley.

But the publicity has not been all bad. Brian Walden, a former Labour Member of Parliament who went on to become an influential TV presenter, raised Myra's case on his Weekend World programme on April 2, 1978. London Weekend TV researchers secured a statement from Maureen Smith which implicated her former husband, David, in the plot to kill Tony Latham.

During his interview, David agreed that he and Ian Brady did hatch the plot. Brian Walden then went on to argue that Smith's testimony against Myra Hindley was crucial. For example, after Edward Evans had been slaughtered with the axe, Myra Hindley – according to David Smith – sat back with a cup of tea, her feet propped up on the mantlepiece, and said: "You should have seen the look on his face, the blow registered in his eyes". And he said that she recalled how, on one occasion, while she was parked on the moors, a police car stopped to enquire if she was having difficulties; Myra was anxious because Ian was over the brow of the hill burying a body.

This testimony was important because it indicated that Myra was a willing accomplice in the murders. The London Weekend programme, however, argued that – because of Smith's conspiracy to murder Latham – doubt was now cast on the reliability of his evidence against Myra. This was nectar to Myra, who knew that she had to turn the public tide in her favour if she was to succeed in her quest for parole.

This televised intervention in the Moors case illustrates the risks of presenting partial evidence in favour of one side of a dispute. David Smith had made a clean breast of the Latham affair to detectives, and the prosecution found no reason to believe that this coloured his evidence. In any event, the photographic and tape recorded evidence clearly implicated Myra in the acts commissioned by Ian Brady.

Arguably, there seems to be poetic justice in Myra Hindley's plight. For if David Smith did not tell the jury at Chester Assizes that he had contemplated the murder of Tony Latham (because he was not asked to do so), she too was singularly silent – over the murder of Pauline Reade, for example. Had Myra been frank with the police, of course, the prosecution would not have needed to rely so heavily on David Smith's evidence; but it is doubtful that her honest disclosures would have justified greater mercy by the court.

* * *

Ian Brady is now resigned to living the rest of his natural life behind bars. That is not an entirely bleak prospect for him, as he noted when he told me about his four years working as a cleaner in Wormwood Scrubbs, in London. This was a golden age for him. He worked in the hospital wing, which brought him into contact with 70 or 80 inmates. He helped them to fill in their parole application forms. He emphasised that, to make a good impression, they needed to stress their "religion, education and family".

"I was in a community for the first time in 12 years," Ian fondly recalls. He met IRA bombers and London gangsters like George Davis and George Ince. Occasionally there was a game of chess to be played. One of his opponents was John Stonehouse, the former Labour Cabinet minister who disgraced himself with financial frauds and then tried to fake his suicide on a Miami beach.

Ian was able to establish a working relationship with the convicts because, while in Parkhurst, he studied psychology. In his first two years in Wormwood Scrubbs he employed self-hypnosis. This, he says, enabled him to weed out his negative traits and reinforce more positive attitudes.

"I knew all the people because I approached them. A lot of them didn't know me: that was the advantage. After maybe five minutes, 10 minutes later, they'd find out who I was, but by then they'd met me, and that was marvellous.

"Anonymity is the most precious thing. The only way to survive in the blocks [solitary confinement in a top security wing] is to get them [prison officers] first: don't wait. That's what I programmed out at the Scrubs. In other words, things that could have provoked me all them years didn't, you know. In fact, I could make friends with a person who tried to provoke. I achieved that facility, that ability. Ability is a better word. Because my approach was reason; reason and under-standing. Understanding their point of view, and their right to their point of view. And their right to their attitude. And still wanting to make friends.

"I kept giving advice – that's the comical thing about it – telling them to pack it in, get a life, keep outside: keep outside, don't waste your life in a garbage can."

There were occasions when he knew he was losing his self-control, when he experienced "bursts" in his head. When this happened, he locked himself in his cell until he regained control.

During his time in Wormwood Scrubs he had the benefit of sustained psychiatric help for two years. He talked about his terrible crimes with someone who offered him therapeutic support.

It came to an end when he was transferred back to Parkhurst. Everyone became his enemy once again. Cut off from the busy, friendly mêlée of a large hospital wing, Ian regressed into a morose and aggressive attitude towards the authorities. He instituted legal proceedings against the government in the European Court of Human Rights, alleging – among other things – that officials were improperly interfering with his mail. And then he was sent to Gartree Prison, which is where I came into the story.

CHAPTER SIXTEEN

The Monster Cried

The tears coursed through the stubble and into the hollows of his cheeks. He was trying to describe one of his homicidal attacks. The eyes were barely open: two slits squinting into the dark recesses of his mind. He peered at a scene so vivid that it was a struggle to expel the words through pursed lips, sharing with me the memories that caused him so much pain.

With his back to the window and the light outside fading fast, the Moors' murderer sat before me in silhouette. It was my sixth visit to Cell 4, and I was still trying to understand how a man could kill so many people. On the basis of what he told me and two psychiatrists I estimate the number at between nine and 12. More than that, I was trying to understand how he could commit sadistic crimes against children. Occasionally Ian Brady became impatient; he wanted me to understand, and expected me to *know* without his having to articulate motives and feelings. But I had to press him for answers. I was not Myra Hindley: there could be no telepathic communication between us.

He did his best. His health was poor; he was now down to under 8 stones, a loss of 5 stones from his normal weight. He had not been to bed for six months. Instead, he reclined in his armchair, nursing into the hollow of his stomach the plastic container filled with warm water. Reclining, but not resting. Nights are the time for vigilance against vengeful Home Office officials who pipe "garbage" through the central heating system in their eternal campaign to wear him down to death. In Ian Brady's world, reality shades off into hallucinatory nightmares.

I knew that his motives were complex. The pre-requisite for

his homicides was the psychotic condition into which he had deteriorated by the age of 17, but from then on his murders break down into three categories.

The first set of killings stemmed from his criminal activities. They were calculated acts of self-preservation, although he still likes to dress them up in dramatic terms. "I had no moral qualms in any criminal matters. It was all to do with getting money as quickly as possible, by any means. Anybody who just happened to get in the way, well it was just too bad. They were totally irrelevant – they would be wiped out. That attitude existed."

The second set of murders occurred when he was in a deranged state. He was trying to illustrate this category of what he calls his "spontaneous" murders when he broke down into tears.

"There was a curious parallel with a dead horse," he said, leaning forward as he drew heavily on a Gauloise. It was the Clydesdale that Ian had seen in agony as it sprawled on the cobbled street in the Gorbals. "I was strolling through a city one night, just soaking up the atmosphere, completely tranquil. Myra was in the city, but I was out on my own. It was dark, and I saw something which brought this image of the horse to my mind."

Brady paused.

Flickering lights, muffled sounds. Something going on behind a car? He walked across and the pain struck him deep, twisting his head, his mouth contorting with the agony of what he saw . . . the Clydesdale lay there, in pain, its big eyes staring frantically at him, appealing for relief, but Ian the boy was helpless.

It was ghastly, but Ian groped forward, hypnotised by the scene of suffering. He reached out. "She had a cloth cap on. She was only an old wino, and I think she told me to 'Fuck off!' But seeing the cap and the hair, I saw the image of the horse . . . the fetlocks, the straggly hair, all wet. Pathetic.

"That's when I went after this other moron. He had been taunting the woman. Looking back he was probably a wino, too. I didn't run after him. I just followed. Waited. And got him."

It was a "capital" killing, he said. He did not make elaborate arrangements for disposing of the body. He just left it there. "I was leaving the city anyway, the next morning," he explained. A body was not buried in God's Garden, but The Face of Death was well satisfied: Ian Brady was "in credit" again.

He repeated this story for me on another occasion; again, he could not suppress the tears, the globs of liquid that testified to the spark of humanity in a man who, in his own words, had over-rated his own callousness.

★   ★   ★

Ian Brady's third category was the ritual murders, cold-blooded, pre-meditated and routinely executed in accordance with the needs of his mad killing cult. These were the child killings, bestial to any right thinking human being. I wanted to know why he did it, and Ian Brady tried to make me understand.

Death was deified in his mad mind. "I have seen death," he told me, "a green face, warm, not unattractive – attractive, in fact. I'll do it a favour, and it will do me favours. Like it will do, in the end. Green, not black – people always associate death with black. The face is not really formed, it's a radiation, a warmth. Warm green."

HARRISON   You do it favours, and it will do you favours?
BRADY   That's the situation now. We all meet it, eventually, and credit's in my favour.
HARRISON   Did the face come to you when you did the killings?
BRADY   Oh yes.
HARRISON   Did the image of death speak to you?
BRADY   I had conversations with it. Everybody has something in them that they converse with, at the purely personal level. Everybody needs something that they are committed to, inside them.

HARRISON   Did you tell Myra about The Face of Death?
BRADY   Oh, she knew everything.

* * *

Because of the complexity of the motives for his murders, it would be a mistake to assume that his three categories fell into distinct compartments. They did not. The child murders, in particular, originated not just as ritual killings, but also because certain events could override the controls over Ian Brady's mind. Christmas was a fatal trigger.

In one psychiatric report his child murders were described as autumnal. Now, it is true that two of the murders for which he was convicted occurred in the autumn, and the third one on December 26; but I was puzzled by the autumnal explanation because it excluded the summertime killings. Was this diagnosis an error?

I came to realise that it was not, when Ian told me about the frequency with which he reads *A Christmas Carol* by Charles Dickens. The story about the mean-spirited Scrooge reveals a great deal about the hollow in Ian Brady's early emotional life. Christmas was a lonely time for Scrooge, for

there he was, alone again, when all the other boys had gone home for the jolly holidays.
He was not reading now, but walking up and down despairingly. Scrooge looked at the Ghost, and with a mournful shaking of his head, glanced anxiously towards the door.
It opened; and a little girl, much younger than the boy, came darting in, and putting her arms about his neck, and often kissing him, addressed him as her 'Dear, dear brother.'
'I have come to bring you home, dear brother!' said the child, clapping her tiny hands, and bending down to laugh. 'To bring you home, home, home!'
'Home, little Fan?' returned the boy.

'Yes!' said the child, brimful of glee. 'Home, for good and all. Home, for ever and ever. Father is much kinder than he used to be. That home's like Heaven! He spoke so gently to me one dear night when I was going to bed, that I was not afraid to ask him once more if you might come home; and he said Yes, you should; and sent me in a coach to bring you. And you're to be a man!' said the child, opening her eyes, and are never to come back here; but first, we're to be together all the Christmas long, and have the merriest time in all the world.' "[1]

Ian Brady enjoyed the Christmas festivities of his childhood. His foster family always placed a stocking at the bottom of his bed filled with gifts. But life turned sour when he found out that he was illegitimate, an outcast from his natural family. "It still mattered, in those days," he told me.

With the passage of years, the story of the birth of Jesus became a reminder that he did not know his father; the Christmas festivities, which meant nothing if they did not celebrate and cement family relationships, were a cruel testament to the fact that he had been denied the security of normal blood bonds with natural mother in those first crucial formative years.

And in his teenage years the lead up to Christmas always seemed to be associated with problems. "Something always happened in the autumn – borstal, remand home – going right back it always happened round about the final three months of the year. I always had a conscious thing about that. Something goes wrong in the final three months." There was one way only to deal with the confluence between his unhappiness and other people's festive cheer, and that was to "destroy" old memories. And this he did by murdering happy children.

If there *was* a God, He had betrayed Ian Stewart. But revenge was sweet, for he could match the birth of Jesus with the

[1] Charles Dickens, *The Christmas Carol*, Harmondsworth; Penguin, Vol. 1, pp. 73–74.

sacrifice of another child. I wanted to know if his heavenward gestures with his defiant clenched-fist were made astride the graves of the children on the moors.

"Yes," he replied solemnly. "So many mistakes."

★　★　★

Ian Brady is one of the tragic figures of our time, a symbol of perversity. He inverted reality. Where normal people express themselves through art, he dared to act. His philosophical justification was an untutored reading of *Crime and Punishment*, which we examined in detail during lengthy discussions in Cell 4.

Dostoyevsky's major novels sought to explore the boundaries of human behaviour. He saw a parallel between his life and his literature. "Everywhere and in everything, I go to the uttermost limit; all my life I have overstepped the mark."[2] Through his fiction he explored the major ethical issues, one of which was the right to kill. And so Raskolnikov explains his motivation to Sonya:

> I wanted to kill without casuistry, to kill for my own sake, for myself alone. I did not want in this matter to lie even to myself. I did not kill to help my mother – that's nonsense. I did not kill in order, having got money and power, to become a benefactor to humanity. Nonsense! I just killed; killed for my own sake, for myself alone . . . Money was not the chief thing I needed when I killed her; it was not money I needed but something else . . . I wanted to know, and to know quickly, whether I was a worm like everyone else, or a man. Shall I be able to transgress or shall I not? Shall I dare to stoop down and take, or not? Am I a trembling creature, or have I the *right*?[3]

[2] Quoted by E.H. Carr, *Dostoevsky*, London: George Allen & Unwin, 1931, pp. 189-90.
[3] *op. cit.*

This reasoning, brutal in its stark simplicity, burnished itself on Ian Brady's ill-formed mind. The words aroused excitement in him, and appeared to legitimise his inclinations.

"What evolved was on a parallel with Raskolnikov," he told me. "It's something that can be done – you can do it – *do it!* Experience it. That was the sort of thing that evolved." Thanks to the endorsement from the pen of the great Russian author, Ian Brady transformed art into life and death. Tragically for his victims, he had failed to absorb the real intent of Raskolnikov's creator.

Dostoyevsky's methodology was analysed by Alfred Adler in a lecture he delivered in Zurich in 1918.

> His principle had been for a long time, even before he gave it expression, *To approach truth through falsehood*, for we never can be certain of possessing truth and have to be prepared to resort to infinitesimal lies.[4]

To test the major ethical issues, Dostoyevsky pushed his characters to the horizons of socially acceptable behaviour. Having reached those limits, however, he and his heroes are amalgamated "with humanity, in deepest humility before God, Czar and Russia. For this feeling that held him in a vice and which might be called the limit-feeling, one which caused him to call a halt, one which had become transformed into a safeguarding feeling of guilt – as his friends often spoke of it – he knew no cause. The hand of God appeared whenever man in over-weaning conceit wished to transcend the limits of his *community-feeling* and warning voices were heard, recommending introspection".[5]

But guilt can operate as a check on behaviour only when a person is able to empathise with others. Ian Brady escaped that constraint because he made a virtue out of being devoid of

---

[4] Alfred Adler, *The Practice and Theory of Individual Psychology*, translator: P. Radin, London: Kegan Paul, Trench, Trubner, 1925 (revised edn 1929), p. 282.
[5] *ibid.*, p. 283.

human feeling. His God, The Face of Death, far from constraining him, by accentuating his social conscience, allured him with the attractions of homicide. He was able to overcome the psychic restraints – personal humility and respect for conventions – that shackle other mortals.

"I reached the stage where, whatever came to mind, get out and do it. Some of it was on the spur of the moment. I led the life that other people would only think about. That's why they are so obsessed with the case for over 20 years. They relate to it: the hideousness, fascinating and horrible."

People, he insisted, were fascinated with the Moors case because they, too, had an "inner darkness". That was why they were afraid: "They are afraid that they can't stop themselves going over the brink and having a glimpse, a vicarious sort of thrill". He had even met people in prison who were curious enough to want the experience of having murdered someone. "They have said 'I'm just going to kill somebody to see what it's like'."

Dostoyevsky explored the unspeakable and plumbed the depths of private error. *Crime and Punishment* was to have included accounts in which girls were sexually violated, sadistically whipped, and murdered, but these descriptions did not appear in the final draft of the manuscript. He used just enough of the right detail to reach an understanding of the nature of Love.

Ian Brady could not speak of love, or write about it. What he could do, however, was translate into action the consequences of the logic that flowed from Raskolnikov's philosophy. He *did* it, and for purely selfish advantage – his salvation after death. But there were also benefits even here on earth. Ian Brady drew sustenance as he squeezed the life forces from his victims. "In the presence of death is life," he explains. "Death always accentuates life."

Brady is not trying to persuade us that he was induced into murder by the awesome power of Dostoyevsky's art. His argument against censorship rests on the claim that "nobody can be corrupted by literature". The arguments marshalled by

Raskolnikov articulated his feelings, and excited him, but he was not thereby induced to kill. "The seed was already there. What was already inside me was expressed there in words. That's why it impressed me. In other words, instead of rambling on for hours trying to express myself, Raskolnikov's situation was a sort of synopsis of precisely how I was. That's what I believed, at that time."

Other fevered minds have also become embroiled in Dostoyevsky's artistic exploration. The first part of the story was published in the *Russian Messenger* in January 1866. Within days, a student in Moscow murdered a usurer and his servant in what looked like a carbon copy killing. "Nature rarely imitates art with such swift precision," notes Steiner[6]. More recently, Nicholas Boyce stunned his wife with a karate chop and strangled her with electric flex. He roasted and baked dismembered parts of the body, which he then concealed in various parts of London. Police found a copy of *Crime and Punishment* in his apartment, in which the arguments in defence of manslaughter were underlined. At his trial, in October 1985, the prosecution was barred from presenting the book, with its highlighted text, as evidence. Boyce was acquitted of murder and sentenced to six years in prison for manslaughter.[7]

*   *   *

Ian Brady now knows that there is more to *Crime and Punishment* than a simple-minded rationalisation for murder. His original acceptance of the Napoleonic thesis – which he summarises as being one in which "there is no God and everything is possible" – was a prescription for anarchy which, if generally pursued, would indeed lead to the Hobbsian nightmare of a brutally short life for everyone.

Even so, his years of solitary reflection have not convinced Brady that moral principles have universal validity. Might, it

[6] Steiner, *op. cit.*, p. 133.
[7] Barry Hugill, 'Perhaps my wife got it wrong', *New Statesman*, October 18, 1985.

seems, is right. That was the way of the world. As evidence, Brady cites the behaviour of Big Business, which has pursued its profits by destroying the Indian tribes of the Amazon basin.

"The first world war was started by a small bunch of privileged people in which millions were killed. There's no such thing as treason, because if you win a war you are not accused of treason. As Herman Goering says, 'The victor decides morality'. Whoever wins dictates morality."

One of his favourite illustrations of what he believes to be the relativity of morality is the British Conservative Party – "a bunch of thieves and murderers. Yet they put themselves up as the party of law and order. They are taking public assets and giving them away to their rich friends on a massive scale that makes the Great Train Robbers look like pick-pockets. It's all a joke, watching these really professional big-time thieves standing on platforms, spouting morality to the masses. They haven't a moral fibre in their bodies. Probably the only book they've read is Machiavelli".

Truth is a plastic value for Ian Brady; it is subjective, so there can be no appeal to an objective reality, no eternal verities to act as guiding touchstones through the treacherous temptations and uncertainties of life.

"What I am saying is that Raskolnikov is Everyman." Ian Brady is hardly qualified to talk for the rest of us, but I pondered on whether he still regarded himself as Raskolnikov's real-life shadow. There was one test to find out.

On several occasions in our discussions he argued that Raskolnikov had over-estimated his callousness. What about Ian Brady? Yes, he too had over-estimated his callousness. Very well, then; was he willing to help the mothers of the children who were still buried on the moors? They wanted their children buried properly in Christian graves, an ambition undiminished despite the passage of over 20 years. Here was the way in which Ian could start to redeem himself in a small way. He had, he said, considered that possibility, and even discussed it with a psychiatrist.

"It's just bringing up ancient history and reviving, opening, old wounds, scars, and nobody is going to gain by it. Nobody."

I tried to persuade him that the mothers would gain by his honest disclosure of what he did with the bodies, but my efforts were fruitless. He would make a clean breast of the facts one day, he said, but when he did so "I will go down". By that, he meant it would be time for him to commit suicide and so terminate his voyage through life. "I have always intended to go by my own volition. And once that [information about his other murders] came out, that would be the incentive."

What troubled him was that new disclosures about his killing cult would upset the few friends who bothered to keep him in touch with the world outside prison, through their correspondence. He could not bear to live with the knowledge that those people, finally, shared his darkest secrets. I argued that there was a therapeutic value in confessing the details about the secret graves; that this would help him to come to terms with his troubled mind. He did not agree. "I find death more attractive than that."

* * *

Ian Brady's biggest mistake was his decision to baptise David Smith into his cult. Why did he set a blood test for a young man who, when it came to murder, had proved himself to be unreliable? A test which, if it failed, could turn into a fatal trap for himself?

"If he failed it, you had no escape, did you?" I asked Ian. "You were putting yourself in a trap. If he failed it, he took you down – which is what happened."

"He didn't fail it," insisted Brady. As far as he was concerned, his hatchet job on Edward Evans proved that his judgment was a correct one. For Smith appeared to remain calm when he was suddenly confronted by the bloody scene in the living room in Wardle Brook Avenue. Smith watched as his friend steadily rained down one blow after another on his victim. Brady scrutinised Smith's reaction. The youth did not panic; he stood his ground, and there was no sign of fear. "His hands were steady, no shakes." Brady held up his right hand to demonstrate his point. "His casualness, wiping up blood, complaining about the blood he had got on his jeans – the normal casualness. I knew he could take it."

Why, then, did he report to the police?

"I think the only reason why he went to the police was the loss of impetus. The body should have been moved out of the house immediately. It would have been all clean, finished. The fact that I hurt my ankle, and was incapacitated . . ." Brady's words trickled away for a few moments, as he dwelt on the event for which he had not planned. Myra made a cup of tea, and the three of them then discussed the arrangments for disposing of the body the following day. Smith went home at about 3 a.m. and was sick. He talked to Maureen until 6 a.m., when he dressed himself and went to a telephone box to raise the alarm.

"What happened in those three hours, I don't know," says Brady, ruminating on his fate yet again. "I would love to know what happened in those three hours. He must have thought that things were getting too hairy. And I think on top of that he had an instinct that I was planning to shoot him." He could not accept the obvious explanation, that – when the chips were down – murder was not on David Smith's agenda.

EPILOGUE

On June 23, 1985, one of my stories in the *Sunday People* declared that 'Broadmoor is the place to send him'. Ian Brady had been fighting for 13 years for a committal to a mental hospital. His requests were repeatedly rejected, despite recommendations from the Home Office's own psychiatrists. Even as a layman, I could see that he was suffering from hallucinations, delusions and paranoid schizophrenia which on humanitarian grounds entitled him to treatment. He did not believe that my disclosures would help to reinforce the expert testimony of psychiatrists.

On August 3, I appealed again to Ian Brady. I told him that his transfer to a mental institution could be linked to his willingness to disclose the whereabouts of the bodies of Pauline Reade and Keith Bennett. I had already been told by the mothers that, in return for this help, they would be pleased to see Brady transferred. And so I wrote to him in these terms: "Even the mothers of Keith Bennett, Pauline Reade and Lesley Ann Downey are now sympathetic to your wish, and they are writing to the Home Office to say so. This is the single most important development in your favour. The Home Office's political objections will be overridden once public support is seen to be reflected by the reaction of these mums".

I argued in these terms: "I believe that I know you better than anyone else, at this precise moment. I believe that you want to redeem yourself, for the most worthy of reasons, but that you can't see how to do so. You feel cornered, and are punishing yourself by saying 'Throw away the key'. That is to your credit. But if anyone can forgive you – then it's the forgiveness of the mums. And I've told you how you can earn that compassion; I have spoken to the mums, and the beginnings of that compassion are already there. Finally, there is another reason why you should now make a clean breast of it: to unburden yourself is the first major step back to mental health".

The media made much of his transfer, for Park Lane is a relatively new hospital where amenities are somewhat better than those to be found in older establishments like Broadmoor. Even his Christmas lunch was front page news! The public was being coaxed into believing that the Moors murderer was getting more than he deserved.

In fact, the reality was different. The psychiatrists knew that, quite apart from his psychoses, Brady had been institutionalised by 20 years in prison; that made him even more difficult to treat. A new regime was established for him which caused some conflict. His armchair was removed from his bedroom, so that he was forced to lie in bed and get a good night's sleep. Brady protested, and the chair was eventually returned – on condition that he did not sleep in it.

Then his braille typewriter was removed from his room. The psychiatrists feared that, for an initial period at any rate, the disturbance to his old routine might heighten the risk of suicide. But Ian was angry: he had used the machine in the privacy of his cell for 17 years without using parts from it as an instrument to draw blood. Despite his annoyance, however, he was told that he would have to use the machine under supervision in the common room.

Despite these initial disruptions to his familiar routine, Brady quickly established a friendly relationship with the nursing staff. They were not "malignant" representatives of the Home Office, but people who might be able to help him with the painful "bursts" in his head.

In March 1986, Ian Brady finally agreed to allow Mrs Ann West, Lesley Ann Downey's mother, to visit him. The long fight to sanity has begun for Ian Brady.

*　★　★*

Lord Longford had two reasons for being delighted with Ian

Brady's transfer to the mental hospital. One was that Brady needed the treatment, and no-one was better qualified to draw this conclusion than the man who had regularly visited him in prison for 15 years. The other reason was that the official recognition that Brady was in need of mental treatment could be interpreteted as a development that favoured Myra Hindley's request for parole.

Myra continues to insist that she was not involved in her lover's misdeeds. This is not what the public believes. People generally assume that she was the stronger character of the pair. That image was fostered at the time of the trial. This is how one author reported his assessment:

> Those who saw Myra in the witness-box agree she was obviously an intelligent, probably tougher character than her lover. Therefore a sinister assumption begins to obtrude itself. Was Myra in fact the dominant partner? When she heard his views and boasts did she, woman-like, say in effect, "Let's not dream and indulge in these fantasies? Let's do something about them. Let's make them real".[1]

This image, which I now regard as a myth, had unfortunate consequences for Myra. It deepened the public's hostility towards her. What Lord Longford characterised as "mob rule" was employed to colour the judgment of the Home Office about whether she should be granted parole.

This depth of public feeling finally drove Hindley's mother to a distressing conclusion. She decided that her daughter – for her own safety's sake – ought never to be granted her freedom; that she ought to die in prison[2]. Perhaps she should; after all, as I have now proved, she committed at least one other murder for which she has yet to stand trial. But it is evidence such as this that should keep her behind bars, rather than the political response to private prejudice.

---

[1] Potter, *op. cit.*, p. 226.
[2] "My Myra should die in prison", *The Sun*, June 20, 1985.

Hot tempers and political expediency have been allowed to intrude on complex penal issues. An example of this was provided by Tom Pendry, the Member of Parliament whose constituency includes Hyde, an area in which Brady and Hindley roamed in search of victims. He told Jimmy Young on his BBC Radio 1 programme on March 1, 1985, that the Moors murders were "So horrifying that the Nuremburg trials pale into insignificance by comparison, in many ways".

Public debate, political decisions and penal policy are not enlightened by such an absurd assessment. Both the Moors murders and the Nuremburg trial exposed the extremes of human depravity, but to assert that the crimes of Brady and Hindley – who were convicted for three murders – were in some qualitative sense worse than the Nazi holocaust that claimed the lives of millions in the most bestial manner, is a travesty that can only be explained in terms of the pursuit of cheap hyperbole.

Even so, Myra Hindley has not helped her own cause. Because she maintains that she is innocent, she cannot also express remorse for the murders which – according to her – she did not commit. More than that, however, she told a reporter in 1985 that she was in love with Ian, rather than "under his spell"[3]. The thesis advanced in this book is that she was, indeed, under a "spell" (of the sort more familiar to psychiatrists than witches, but either way a spell which acknowledged that she had lost a degree of self-control over her actions). If Myra is right, if she was *not* under a spell, then the degree of her culpability for the sadistic murder of children is even greater.

Myra has now found a literary agent, and she is writing her memoirs. It remains to be seen whether her book is an honest confession or a nauseating *apologia*.

* * *

[3] Peter Francis, "Inside the mind of Myra Hindley", *Chat*, January 18, 1986.

Without David Smith, the Moors murders might never have come to light; or at the very least, other children would have died before fate intervened to put a stop to the killing cult. The legacy of the trial, however, has been 20 years of nightmare for Smith. People in Manchester, far from thanking him for his intervention, immediately assumed that he must have been more deeply involved than was admitted at Chester Assizes. The result is that he is now in self-imposed exile from most of the pubs around Dukinfield, where he lives, because of the whispers and hostile looks directed against him and his family.

He has refused to change his name (people usually adopt the name of Smith when they want anonymity) or move out of the district. So far as murder is concerned, his conscience is clear: so why should he go on the run from his home town? This bellicose attitude occasionally leads to new fist fights, though these are becoming less frequent now (which is just as well, because his permanently swollen right hand with its fractured bones cannot now be used to administer uppercuts with the vigour of his youth).

David Smith makes no apologies for the behaviour of his teenage years, but nor will he censure people who harbour unfounded suspicions against him: "If I was Joe Soap, I wouldn't want to live next door to David Smith," he asserts disarmingly. Deep down, however, he feels hurt that he – and particularly his loyal wife, Mary, and his four children – should have turned into victims of the Moors murderers' reputations.

"I can never stop people's suspicions of me, but one day I hope their opinions develop from the truth and not rumours – or worse still, from the great unsaid. You know the idea – no matter what is said, or whatever 'comes out', there *must* have been more. More what, for Christ sake? More involvement? More evil? More just because they *want* more!!

"I'm tired of it every year, very very tired. I want an end to it, one way or the other. I don't need to add to my life: I have all I ever wanted, my wife and my family. I don't care one bit about what is rumoured or thought about me, just as long as it is all based on the truth. If I'm still hated, then so be it; in fact in private moments of thought I'm not over-fond of myself."

Finding a job has proved difficult for David Smith, so he remains at home administering to his family's domestic needs while Mary goes to work. He has mellowed with age, but even now he will resort to the old techniques for settling disputes. I visited him in Strangeways Prison on September 25, 1985, where he was serving a month's confinement for contempt of court. While standing outside Machester Crown Court, he butted a witness with his head in an altercation that he accepted had serious implications. "You can't do that to witnesses in court," he said with a grin, "it's an attack on the Establishment."

Smith agreed to be completely frank with me in the hope that a definitive account of his association with Brady and Hindley would at last enable him to close that chapter of his life.

"You asked why I was affected by Evans when I myself used weapons and violence without much thought. I don't know an easy answer. I don't even know if there is one. I know the buzz and the teasing had instantly stopped. My violence was used to beat and win. With Evans they hammered him while his only defence was to scream for his mother. I know my mistakes: one of them isn't hammering some kid fourteen times with an axe.

"In others' eyes I might well be a walking shithouse, but in my eyes before I go to bed I know I have never murdered. Brady made one massive mistake, and that's it. After the arrest, the bits and pieces all came together – what was boozy conversations about 'others' and 'photographic proof' suddenly struck home and became not idle boasts but reality. Obviously (and rightly) the police viewed me with suspicion. On matters away from the Evans case they gave me a rough time.

"Twenty years later I still contemplate two matters. (1) If Evans had been Latham, how would I have reacted, and how would the future have developed between the three of us? (2) If Evans had been buried and I had accepted the act, what next? It's difficult for me to accept the three of us setting out on a spree of butchery, oblivious to thoughts of discovery and capture. To my mind, a group of three bonded together by crime would inevitably lead to suspicion, rivalry, and a weak link. If faced with a choice, I would have wanted her to be viewed as a weak link. Twenty years later, the thought that these things might well have become my future still gives me the shits.

"I feel sick with thoughts that Brady not only killed individuals, one after another, he also unforgivably killed the future for those left behind, and for those never to be born. By killing one, he killed generations, and by that he has desecrated the future."

On November 23, 1985 – coincidentally, exactly 22 years after the disappearance of John Kilbride – I drove David Smith around the moors of Lancashire and Derbyshire. We were searching for the spots to which he had been driven by Myra Hindley. He was told by Brady that he had stood near a child's grave on at least one of these locations. It was a fruitless journey, but Smith – now driven by Mary – has resolved to keep searching with the police until, with luck, he might one day discover the graves of Keith Bennett and Pauline Reade.

APPENDIX

On the Law

My first contact with the mind of Ian Brady was early in 1983, when I was shown a letter in which he had written his observations on the Falklands war between Britain and Argentina. One passage in particular was blood-curdling. It set out his image of the Prime Minister, Margaret Thatcher:

> My favourite image of what her "new spirit of Britain" opportunistic drivel inspires in me: I imagine her giving her "royal" waves on the steps of No. 10 – her scalp suddenly disintegrates like a rotten turnip, ending up on the pavement, resembling the fur of a newly-skinned rabbit and her blood-spouting trunk buckles backward to join it in its rightful place – the gutter. *That* would really be "the new spirit of Britain" – an "enterprising" individual with some initiative and a magazine of hollow-nosed, high-velocity bullets!

Here was a sick mind. The psychiatrist to whom I showed the letter drew the conclusion that Brady had cast Mrs Thatcher in the rôle of his mother, on whom he wreaks revenge.

The loss of a parent is a crucial part of the explanation why some people are prone to depression and personality disorders. Children in this situation adopt either neurotic disorders or delinquent behaviour, which serve as a "permanent diversion" from the emotions caused by this loss. We do not yet know enough about the impact of such loss to be able to predict how particular individuals will be affected, so we have to settle for general statements such as this one:

. . . the particular pattern of depressive disorder that a person develops will turn on the particular pattern of childhood experiences he has had, and also on the nature and circumstances of the adverse event he has recently experienced.[1]

Ian Brady lost his father, and had an unsatisfactory relationship with his mother. He became a psychopath. David Smith lost his mother, and had an unsatisfactory relationship with his father. He became an anti-social delinquent. Of course, in each case, other social and environmental factors contributed to the eventual outcome, but of one thing we can be confident: the growing tendency in the western world towards one-parent families is storing up trouble that will manifest itself in psychological and criminal traumas for an increasing number of people.[2] That is why we need to critically re-examine the socio-medical and legal mechanisms for rehabilitating the victims of this change in the structure of the family.

Ian Brady's case exposes the inability of the British legal system to deal with a person who is mentally ill but not criminally insane. Our critique of that system is consistent with the evidence now rapidly accumulating that demonstrates the need for a substantial revision in the system itself – ironically, along the lines of the Napoleonic Code.

Brady was suffering from a variety of pyschotic disorders when I first met him, and he had been in that state for many years; yet he was not being treated. Two strong recommendations had been made by Home Office-approved psychiatrists that he ought to be transferred to a mental hospital. The first one was made as a result of an examination of Brady's case by

[1] John Bowlby, *Attachment and Loss*, Vol. III, London: Hogarth Press, 1980, p. 248.
[2] In Britain there were about 900,000 one-parent families in 1981. About one in eight of all families with dependent children are headed by one parent, predominantly mothers (87%). About 1.5m children are involved.

Dr Peter Scott in 1971. The politicians, however, refused to act on the recommendation by Scott, who was acknowledged as "one of this country's most distinguished forensic psychiatrists" by Lord Elton, the Minister of State at the Home Office.[3]

Few people familiar with Brady's case had any doubts about why this, and a subsequent recommendation, were not accepted. For example, during the course of an interview, a psychiatrist asked me not to identify him or the contents of the report that he had prepared on Brady, because disclosure would probably lead to unfavourable publicity. The outcome, he said, would probably be that – once again – Brady would be denied appropriate treatment. His case, said the psychiatrist, was "an exquisitely political one".

Surely no political consideration is strong enough to override a person's right to medical treatment? Outlaws are properly deprived of their civil liberties, but they do not lose all of their basic human rights (once the decision to abolish capital punishment has been taken). That principle, however, was not acknowledged in Brady's case.

We have here, then, a further argument for some fundamental reforms to Anglo-American jurisprudence. This system is based on the adversarial approach to justice, which is now seen to be notoriously deficient in its ability to deliver justice to both the innocent and the guilty. The main thrust of the criticism has been directed at the miscarriages of justice (see, for example, the exposés by Ludovic Kennedy, the British broadcaster and writer[4]). Innocent people have been sent to the gallows, or spent years in prison for crimes they did not commit. In his 25 years as secretary of *Justice*, Tom Sargant investigated many miscarriages of justice in the British courts. "I have come to the conclusion that far from being the best

---

[3] *Hansard*, December 12, 1984, col. 370.

[4] Kennedy's most recent critique of the Anglo-American system appears in his re-assessment of the evidence against Richard Hauptmann, who was executed for allegedly killing Charles Lindberg's baby. See *The Airman and the Carpenter*, London: Collins, 1985.

system in the world, it is worse than many of the other systems in western Europe".[5]

The inquisitorial system employed by the French, based on the examining magistrate, is increasingly recognised as superior to the Anglo-American system. Napoleon bequeathed the *Juge d'instruction* to his countrymen as an independent inquisitor who would have powers to establish truth; to this end, he combines some of the powers of both judge and police.[6]

Of particular significance for us here is The Mental Health Act of Ontario, Canada, the operation of which has been summarised by Mr Justice Edson Haines of the High Court of Justice of Ontario.

> . . . it is the concept of our statute that the rights of the mentally ill patient, his protection and that of the public are altogether too precious and delicate to be entrusted solely to an adversary system. Therefore, while preserving the essential elements of the adversary system, there has been engrafted upon it an inquisitorial system where the Advisory Review Board has the advantage of having on it two independent, skilled psychiatrists who examine the patient and make themselves fully aware of his medical condition.[7]

This "happy amalgamation of the inquisitorial and adversary systems", if it had been in operation in Britain, would probably have been fairer for both Ian Brady and the families whose children were not unearthed by the police. Brady would have ended up in a mental institution, which would have ensured

[5] Tom Sargant, 'The court of expediency', *New Society*, May 2, 1985.
[6] This is not to say that the Napoleonic Code is the final word on justice; it is not. The French spent a great deal of legislative time during 1985 in preparing the groundwork for a substantial revision of the rules governing their 552 examining magistrates.
[7] Mr Justice Haines, 'Psychiatry and the Adversary System of Justice', in David N. Weisstub, editor, *Law and Psychiatry*, New York: Pergamon, 1978, p.122.

immediate treatment for his psychoses. And in that therapeutic environment, I am convinced that he would have been willing to confess formally to upwards of nine other murders (not all of them involving Myra Hindley) – providing a merciful release from uncertainty for many families.

Brady did not have confidence in his jailers, and was not willing to cooperate with a frank confession when (as he saw it) he was doomed to nothing but incarceration. Yet there was so much to discover, as I learnt when I asked him the date on which he committed his first killing.

BRADY   I can go back to the age of about eight in the Gorbals.

HARRISON   About what?

BRADY   About what we are talking about.

HARRISON   How do you mean?

BRADY   I can go back that far, 8, 9 years old.

HARRISON   Ian, I don't understand what you mean. You weren't doing those things then? Why do you say that?

BRADY   This was an accident. Going right back then, and I don't know the result – whether death occurred as a result of that, because I've forgotten things as quickly as possible.

HARRISON   What, when you were 8-years-old?

BRADY   Yes.

HARRISON   Someone died then, did they?

BRADY   They were so strong, they must have . . . you know, and it was an accident.

It was garbled, but Brady – believing that it was not necessary to articulate all his thoughts – wanted me to understand that he was associated with a death at the early age of 8. I wanted to press him with more specific questions, but at this point the afternoon tea was delivered to Cell 4: the spell of the moment was broken, and my questions would have to remain unanswered until another occasion.

Unfortunately, there was not to be another occasion. On June 27, 1985, I received a letter from the Governor of Gartree

Prison. Acting on instructions from the Home Office, he forthwith banned me from further visits to Ian Brady because I had dared to write an article about one of their prisoners.

The trial of the Moors murderers raised more questions than it answered, but it was not incumbent on the judge and jury to search for answers to questions such as whether Brady had, in fact, killed another 9 people, and why he had killed in the first place. The truth that emerged in the court at Chester Assizes was relative to the rules of the legal game. Those rules need to be modified, so that the community can be provided with something approximating the objective truth.

POSTSCRIPT

The Brainwashing of Myra Hindley

A remarkable conspiracy was triggered by the publication of this book. A detective, a Methodist minister, a lawyer and I joined forces to help Myra Hindley to confess to the murders of Pauline Reade and Keith Bennett.

For 20 years Hindley shielded her mind from the horrendous deeds that she and her lover, Ian Brady, had perpetrated. She preserved her sanity by convincing herself that the sadistic torture and murder of three young people had nothing to do with her – and that she certainly had no responsibility for a further two deaths.

The conspirators, each working in his own principled way, knew that many layers of self-delusion had to be washed from Hindley's brain if the files on two Missing Persons – a 12-year-old boy with horn-rimmed spectacles and a cheeky grin, and a blossoming 16-year-old girl – were to be closed. The collaboration was not prearranged. It was a loose-knit confederation that was articulated by fast-moving circumstances which thrust everyone towards the truth; the truth that would finally banish the anguish of uncertainty which afflicted two mothers.

This concerted attack on Hindley in her lair in Cookham Wood Prison was all the more astonishing because two of the conspirators – the minister and the lawyer – were members of the Hindley "camp". They had to represent her pleas of innocence to a cynical public. But at no stage did they offend against their consciences or codes of ethics. They were committed to the best interests of the most hated woman in Britain: but they saw that, working *with* Myra Hindley, the truth would eventually be in her best psychological and penal interests. Their work with Hindley was accomplished within the framework and pace established by the two investigators, the detective and the journalist.

For three of the players in this delicate psychological drama the path towards truth was strewn with snipers. The minister, the Reverend Peter Timms, was obstructed by the Home Office. The lawyer, Michael Fisher, was placed under pressure to restrain his enthusiasm by some of Hindley's influential well-wishers. And the detective, Chief Superintendent Peter Topping, was attacked by Members of Parliament and Fleet Street newspapers for staging a "media circus" on Saddleworth moor. None of them lost their nerve.

Between February 19 and 24, 1987, ten months after the publication of *Brady & Hindley: Genesis of the Moors Murders*, in an interview room strewn with maps and photographs, Myra Hindley formally confessed to the murder of Pauline Reade and Keith Bennett. The British public received the news with relief. At the same time, people were sceptical about Hindley's motives. Few believed that she was sincere in her expressions or remorse. She was still regarded as the calculating killer who was exploiting an opportunity for her own advantage. This was a wrong perception, but an understandable one: for the public had to be kept in the dark about what was going on behind the scenes. Premature publicity would have placed Myra Hindley on her guard, and she would have probably taken the last ugly secrets of the Moors Murders to her grave.

The campaign to make Myra talk acquired a momentum that was almost unstoppable, once I published Doreen Wright's testimony. But Hindley did not give in without a struggle.

She denied admitting – in a moment of rage – being a party to the killing of Pauline Reade. Ian Brady, the man with whom she connived in that murder, mischievously confided in a letter to Lord Longford that "I know Myra, she wouldn't make the mistake of uttering such a statement". It does not take a student of the Oxford school of linguistic philosophy to

realise that this was not a denial, but a coded admission that
there was a mistake to be made – as David Smith was quick to
note. Myra Hindley *had* made the mistake. But the ever-
gallant Lord Longford, invited by Granada Television to
comment on the evidence in this book, disparaged Miss
Wright's testimony as "absolute drivel". He impugned me as
an "unreliable figure". The chief of detectives, reading the
book in his eighth floor office in Chester House, the nerve
centre of Manchester's police force, arrived at a different
conclusion.

Mr Topping, the 46-year-old father of two daughters,
brooded on the problem for several days. He was now in
charge of a case that would not go away; one that had dark
and mysterious undertones and sensitive political overtones.
He was a uniformed Bobby in the police division which was
responsible for the original search when Pauline Reade was
reported missing; and here he was, a generation later, confronted with a tactical choice that would determine the
outcome of the most notorious case of murder in modern
criminal history.

Mr Topping had tried the direct approach with Brady.
Following the publication of my stories that Brady had
confessed to the murders, the detective drove down to Gartree
Prison in the hope of extracting a formal confession. Brady
remained his stoic self. A similar straight-up approach to
Myra Hindley would probably be just as futile. She would
have to be stalked. The manpower at Mr Topping's disposal
was already stretched; in particular, he was handling the
delicate investigation into allegations against John Stalker,
his Deputy Chief Constable. But in any event the secrecy that
was crucial to the solution of this crime dictated the need for
a very small unit of detectives. He selected Geoff Knupfer, a
38-year-old inspector, and Gordon Mutch, the 36-year-old
father of two sons.

As Mr Topping was making his operational decisions,
Peter Timms and I were invited to the BBC studios at
Broadcasting House, London. Radio 4 recorded a programme

in which we discussed Hindley's "confession", her moral obligations to tell the truth and her prospects for parole. Mr Timms, a former governor of one of H.M. Prisons, tended to accept Hindley's professions of innocence; was she not converted to the Roman Catholic faith? Mr Timms advocated her case and favoured forgiveness. Once the microphones were switched off, I invited Mr Timms to consider a problem: if Myra *was* telling the truth, then a respectable woman, the former nurse at Holloway Prison, was a liar. And I suggested that, during their next meeting, Mr Timms should put a certain question to Myra – and look deep into her eyes when she answered.

It was not Mr Timm's job to sit in judgment on Myra Hindley. He had been invited to visit her by the prison's Catholic priest, but he had no official standing. He could only listen to Hindley, and offer counsel if she sought it. Even so, Mr Timms was acutely aware that two families in Manchester were suffering for the want of knowledge about the fate of their children.

The minister determined to see the tragedy through to the end. But he reckoned without the bureaucrats: he was not allowed to visit her on a regular basis, to engage in that painfully protracted therapy that sometimes enables a person to unlock the deepest secrets from a haunted mind. He received a taste of the red-tape that had locked me out of Ian Brady's cell.

Mr Timms later recalled for me: "During the last 18 months it's been one hell of a struggle, from one battle to another, to see her and help her through it. Had I been allowed to see her after talking to you, after that radio programme, I have not the slightest doubt that this matter would have been resolved months and months earlier. I was stopped from seeing her. If I had been a Catholic priest, it would have been OK. The whole thing was so bloody awful, it wasn't true. In the end I thought 'What's this all about?' I wasn't in it for kicks."

* * *

As the summer of '86 progressed, the Topping team worked away. First, all the original evidence was gathered up. They scoured the files of neighbouring police forces and traced retired policemen to their country cottages, to assemble documents, photographs and exhibits which eventually filled 13 cardboard boxes.

Then the material was painstakingly reassessed for vital clues which the original investigators might have overlooked. Old witnesses were reinterviewed, and as the dragnet grew wider the risk of publicity increased. I monitored the moves, not least because Mrs Winnie Johnstone, Keith Bennett's mother, regularly telephoned me late at night to ask about progress. At a meeting in Mr Topping's office, I agreed to keep a lid on what was by any standards a sensational story.

The gumshoe strategy started to produce results. Photographs extracted from Brady's tartan album helped to identify some of the couple's secret picnic spots. David Smith provided corroborative information. Another turn-up for the book was the discovery that Philip Deare was *not* murdered by Ian Brady: after the two borstal chums went their separate ways, Deare gravitated to London where he worked as a steel erector and became an alcoholic. He drowned in a Sheffield lake in 1977, and was buried in a pauper's grave.

The autumn advanced, and the time drew near for a showdown with Myra Hindley. I was invited to a meeting with Mr Topping and his two detectives on November 14. To avoid a "leak" I was asked not to go to his office in Chester House. Instead, we met in the Seymour Suite in the nearby Trafford Hall Hotel. I was asked not to publish my scoop because the element of surprise was crucial. Some gaps in the information had not been plugged, but I was asked not to identify them – for as Mr Knupfer put it, if Brady and Hindley read about the weaknesses in the police case "they would be laughing at us". The detectives had orchestrated a psychological approach to Myra Hindley which was designed to tilt her in the direction of cooperation; bluff was one of their weapons. Secret arrangements were made with the

Prison Department at the Home Office to ensure that knowledge about the visit was even withheld from officers at Cookham Wood. The stealthy approach began to pay off. "Come on, Myra!" I wrote in my diary for Monday, November 17. Sitting outside the Kent prison, I saw the unmarked squad car pull up at the gates. It was early: 1.15 p.m. Sgt Mutch swiftly turned his wheels and retreated into the centre of Rochester. At precisely 2 p.m. the black saloon cruised up the road and stopped in front of the gates. Out stepped Mr Topping and Mr Knupfer. Myra Hindley was taken aback. She was already unnerved by a moving letter which she had received from Mrs Johnstone, and when confronted by the soft-spoken chief superintendent and his new evidence, she broke down and agreed to help.

Mr Topping could not believe his luck. Myra Hindley invited him to return the following day with maps and photographs, so that she could try and identify locations that the police ought to search. She would not admit to being involved in the murders; but she longed for the suffering to end, and wanted to help. The detectives were elated: Myra Hindley had cracked.

But it was an intense haul forward to the confession.

As the police sniffer dogs searched the moors for the graves, Michael Fisher gently guided Hindley and openly responded to questions from the media. He had formed a view on how to best serve Myra's interests which did not meet with the wholehearted approval of some of Hindley's influential friends. They had long believed that her predicament was of Fleet Street's making; and that the best strategy was to silence the newspapers, so that one day the Home Office would be able to quietly free her.

Mr Fisher did not agree. Nor did he think it was in Myra's interests to paint her as Miss Goody Two Shoes. Consultations took place to decide what to do about him. He could not be directly gagged, so Lord Goodman, the former Master of University College, Oxford, and legal adviser to some of the country's High and Mighty leaders, was asked to adjudicate.

Mr Fisher was invited to a breakfast conference at Lord Goodman's Regent's Park apartment. He explained his attitude and his frank approach to the media – during TV interviews, for example, he had acknowledged that Myra's 20-year silence was indefensible. The whole affair was not Fleet Street's fault, argued Mr Fisher. He pointed out that Brady and Hindley were responsible for starting the story, and that the only way forward for Myra was for her to make a clean breast of it.

Lord Goodman, sitting at the top of the breakfast table, reached his judgment. He said that it was plain that Myra would never be released, and he agreed that, once Fleet Street newspapers had got their teeth into a story, there was no way of silencing them. His view was that Fisher's route, that Myra should do everything possible to help the police, was the correct one; and that the solicitor should be left to use that argument on Myra's behalf.

"If Lord Goodman, the most eminent solicitor in the country, had gone against me, I think Myra would have received a letter from several people telling her to change her solicitor," recalled Mr Fisher. He had won; and when Lord Longford was asked to appear on Terry Wogan's television chat show, *he* was the one invited to remain silent about Myra Hindley.

The strain of reliving her harrowing past began to tell on Hindley. She started taking double doses of Valium, and she focused her anger on me. "That Fred Harrison!" she declared to Mr Fisher. " I wouldn't be in this situation if it wasn't for him."

But the strategy had worked, and on December 7, 1986, in *Sunday Today* – under a headline which declared "I'm Guilty" – I reported that Myra Hindley had admitted: "Everyone thinks that at the end of the day I am going to blame everything on Brady. But I am not going to do that".

The rest is history. Myra Hindley was escorted back to Saddleworth moor on December 16, where she pointed out spots that were of particular interest to Ian Brady.

David Smith followed three days later. He was not warned that the police were going to take him up onto the moor, and he was only clad in "dancing shoes" as he stepped into snow that was banked two-feet high around the police caravan. Jostling photographers did little to soften his mood, and he had a stand-up row with Mr Topping. When Mr Smith threatened to walk out, the Chief Superintendent warned him: "You'll walk all the way back home". A blizzard was raging outside. Mr Knupfer diplomatically leaned against the caravan door and calmed Mr Smith down.

Mr Stalker, who had by now been exonerated and returned to his duties as Deputy Chief Constable, could not be placated. He announced his resignation on December 19. One of his reasons was the fact that he had not been briefed about the Hindley visit.

Hindley ruminated on her position over Christmas, and Mr Timms was encouraged to pay her regular visits. He agreed, on the condition that the visits would be allowed to continue so long as Myra wanted them – a deal on which the Home Office reneged, once Hindley had confessed.

Mr Stalker appeared on Terry Wogan's show to say that, given his knowledge and experience, he would have "handled the case differently". Mr Topping's strategy, however, had been vindicated: he already had Myra Hindley's signature on a confession. Mr Stalker did not know about it, because Messrs Topping, Fisher and Timms had made a pact to clamp down on publicity until the graves were found.

Lord Longford, while declaring that he would not have advised Myra to accept "equal" responsibility for the killings, was moved to forgive me for restarting the investigation in the first place.

April 20, 1987

True crime – now available in paperback from Grafton Books

Professor Keith Simpson
Forty Years of Murder (illustrated) £2.95 ☐

Vincent Teresa
My Life in the Mafia £2.50 ☐

Robert Jackson
Francis Camps £1.95 ☐

John Camp
100 Years of Medical Murder (illustrated) £2.50 ☐

Colin Wilson
A Criminal History of Mankind £3.95 ☐

Stephen Knight
Jack the Ripper: The Final Solution (illustrated) £2.95 ☐
The Killing of Justice Godfrey (illustrated) £2.95 ☐

Peter Maas
The Valachi Papers £2.50 ☐

John Pearson
The Profession of Violence (illustrated) £2.95 ☐

Sir Sydney Smith
Mostly Murder (illustrated) £2.95 ☐

Stewart Tendler and David May
The Brotherhood of Eternal Love (illustrated) £2.50 ☐

Roger Wilkes
Wallace: The Final Verdict (illustrated) £2.50 ☐

To order direct from the publisher just tick the titles you want
and fill in the order form.

Crime fiction – now available in paperback from Grafton Books

To order direct from the publisher just tick the titles you want
and fill in the order form.   **GF2681**

War – now available in paperback from Grafton Books

Alexander Baron		
From the City, From the Plough	£1.95	☐
Norman Mailer		
The Naked and the Dead	£2.95	☐
Tim O'Brien		
If I Die in a Combat Zone	£1.95	☐
James Webb		
Fields of Fire	£2.95	☐
A Sense of Honour	£2.95	☐
John McAleer and Billy Dickson		
Unit Pride	£2.50	☐
J P W Mallalieu		
Very Ordinary Seaman	£1.95	☐
Nicholas Monsarrat		
HMS Marlborough Will Enter Harbour	£1.50	☐
Three Corvettes	£1.50	☐
Dan van der Vat		
The Last Corsair (illustrated)	£2.50	☐
The Ship that Changed the World (illustrated)	£3.50	☐
Erich Maria Remarque		
All Quiet on the Western Front	£2.50	☐
Robert Kee		
A Crowd Is Not Company	£1.95	☐
Etty Hillesum		
Etty: A Diary 1941–3	£2.50	☐
Leon Uris		
Battle Cry	£2.95	☐

To order direct from the publisher just tick the titles you want
and fill in the order form.   **GF1981**

True war – now available in paperback from Grafton Books

To order direct from the publisher just tick the titles you want
and fill in the order form.

Crime fiction – now available in paperback from Grafton Books

To order direct from the publisher just tick the titles you want and fill in the order form.

GF2781

War fiction – now available in paperback from Grafton Books

C S Forester
The Gun   95p ☐

Alexander Fullerton
Surface!   £1.50 ☐
The Waiting Game   £1.50 ☐

Leon Uris
Battle Cry   £2.95 ☐

Len Deighton
Bomber   £2.95 ☐
Declarations of War   £2.50 ☐
Goodbye Mickey Mouse   £2.95 ☐

James Webb
Fields of Fire   £2.95 ☐
A Sense of Honour   £2.95 ☐

Erich Maria Remarque
All Quiet on the Western Front   £2.50 ☐

To order direct from the publisher just tick the titles you want
and fill in the order form.   **GF2281**

The best of crime fiction now available in paperback from Grafton Books

John Hutten

Accidental Crimes	£1.95	☐
29 Herriott Street	£1.95	☐

Dan Kavanagh

Duffy	£1.50	☐
Fiddle City	£1.50	☐

Joseph Hansen

Troublemaker	£2.50	☐
Fade Out	£2.50	☐
Gravedigger	£1.95	☐
Skinflick	£1.95	☐
The Man Everybody was Afraid of	£1.95	☐
Nightwork	£1.95	☐

Stephen Knight

Requiem at Rogano	£2.50	☐

Rod Miller

The Animal Letter	£2.50	☐

To order direct from the publisher just tick the titles you want
and fill in the order form.

True war – now available in paperback from Grafton Books

Alexander Baron		
From the City, From the Plough	£1.95	☐
C S Forester		
Hunting the Bismarck	£1.50	☐
Ka-Tzetnik		
House of Dolls	£2.50	☐
Olga Lengyel		
Five Chimneys	£1.95	☐
Dr Miklos Nyiszli		
Auschwitz	£1.95	☐
Alexander McKee		
Dresden 1945 (illustrated)	£2.50	☐
F Spencer-Chapman		
The Jungle is Neutral [illustrated]	£2.50	☐
Bryan Perrett		
Lightning War: A History of Blitzkrieg (illustrated)	£2.95	☐
Leonce Péillard		
Sink the Tirpitz!	£1.95	☐
Richard Pape		
Boldness Be My Friend (illustrated)	£2.50	☐
Baron Burkhard von Mullenheim-Rechberg		
Battleship Bismarck (illustrated)	£3.50	☐
Livia E Bitton Jackson		
Elli: Coming of Age in the Holocaust	£2.50	☐
Charles Whiting		
Siegfried: The Nazis' Last Stand (illustrated)	£2.50	☐
First Blood: The Battle of the Kasserine Pass 1943 (illustrated)	£2.50	☐

To order direct from the publisher just tick the titles you want
and fill in the order form.

The world's greatest thriller writers now
available in paperback from Grafton Books

Len Deighton

Twinkle, Twinkle, Little Spy	£2.50	☐
Yesterday's Spy	£1.95	☐
Spy Story	£2.50	☐
Horse Under Water	£2.50	☐
Billion Dollar Brain	£2.50	☐
The Ipcress File	£2.50	☐
An Expensive Place to Die	£2.50	☐
Declarations of War	£2.50	☐
SS-GB	£2.50	☐
XPD	£2.95	☐
Bomber	£2.95	☐
Fighter (non-fiction)	£2.95	☐
Blitzkrieg (non-fiction)	£2.50	☐
Funeral in Berlin	£2.50	☐
Goodbye Mickey Mouse	£2.95	☐

'Game, Set and Match' Series

Berlin Game	£2.95	☐
Mexico Set	£2.95	☐
London Match	£2.95	☐

Jack Higgins

A Game for Heroes	£1.95	☐
The Wrath of God	£1.95	☐
The Khufra Run	£1.95	☐
Bloody Passage	£1.95	☐

Trevanian

The Loo Sanction	£2.50	☐
The Eiger Sanction	£2.50	☐
Shibumi	£2.50	☐
The Summer of Katya	£1.95	☐

To order direct from the publisher just tick the titles you want
and fill in the order form.

The most chilling horror stories – now available in paperback from Grafton Books

Robert Bloch		
The Night of the Ripper	£2.50	☐
Richard Haigh		
The Farm	£1.75	☐
The City	£1.95	☐
Michael Shea		
The Colour out of Time	£1.95	☐
Mendal Johnson		
Let's Go Play at the Adams'	£2.50	☐
H P Lovecraft		
Omnibus 1: At the Mountains of Madness	£2.95	☐
Omnibus 2: Dagon and other macabre tales	£2.95	☐
Omnibus 3: The Haunter of the Dark	£2.95	☐
Brian Lumley		
Psychomech	£1.95	☐
Psychosphere	£1.95	☐
Psychamok	£2.50	☐
Necroscope	£3.50	☐
Whitley Strieber		
Black Magic	£1.95	☐
The Night Church	£1.95	☐
Miles Gibson		
The Sandman	£1.95	☐
Ramsey Campbell		
The Nameless	£1.95	☐
The Parasite	£2.50	☐
Incarnate	£2.50	☐
Obsession	£2.50	☐

To order direct from the publisher just tick the titles you want
and fill in the order form.   **GF3181**

The world's greatest thriller writers now
available in paperback from Grafton Books

Anthony Price

Soldier No More	£2.50	☐
The Old Vengeful	£2.50	☐
Gunner Kelly	£1.95	☐
Sion Crossing	£2.50	☐
Here Be Monsters	£2.50	☐

Julian Rathbone

A Spy of the Old School	£1.95	☐
Nasty, Very	£2.50	☐

Matthew Heald Cooper

To Ride A Tiger	£2.50	☐
When Fish Begin to Smell	£1.95	☐

Donald Seaman

The Wilderness of Mirrors	£2.50	☐

Dan Sherman

The Prince of Berlin	£1.95	☐

To order direct from the publisher just tick the titles you want
and fill in the order form.

All these books are available at your local bookshop or newsagent, or can be ordered direct from the publisher.

To order direct from the publishers just tick the titles you want and fill in the form below.

Name _____

Address _____

Send to:
Grafton Cash Sales
PO Box 11, Falmouth, Cornwall TR10 9EN.

Please enclose remittance to the value of the cover price plus:

UK 60p for the first book, 25p for the second book plus 15p per copy for each additional book ordered to a maximum charge of £1.90.

BFPO 60p for the first book, 25p for the second book plus 15p per copy for the next 7 books, thereafter 9p per book.

Overseas including Eire £1.25 for the first book, 75p for second book and 28p for each additional book.

Grafton Books reserve the right to show new retail prices on covers, which may differ from those previously advertised in the text or elsewhere.